Second Workshop on Bridging Human-Computer Interaction and Natural Language Processing (HCI+NLP 2022)

Online
15 July 2022

ISBN: 978-1-7138-5634-4

Printed from e-media with permission by:

Curran Associates, Inc.
57 Morehouse Lane
Red Hook, NY 12571

CURRAN ASSOCIATES INC. proceedings .com

Some format issues inherent in the e-media version may also appear in this print version.

Association for Computational Linguistics
209 N. Eighth Street
Stroudsburg, Pennsylvania 18360

Phone: 1-570-476-8006
Fax: 1-570-476-0860

acl@aclweb.org

Additional copies of this publication are available from:

Curran Associates, Inc.
57 Morehouse Lane
Red Hook, NY 12571 USA
Phone: 845-758-0400
Fax: 845-758-2633
Email: curran@proceedings.com
Web: www.proceedings.com

HCI+NLP 2022

Second Workshop on Bridging Human–Computer Interaction and Natural Language Processing

Proceedings of the Workshop

July 15, 2022

The HCI+NLP organizers gratefully acknowledge the support from the following sponsors.

Sponsored by

Adobe

Microsoft

Order copies of this and other ACL proceedings from:

Association for Computational Linguistics (ACL)
209 N. Eighth Street
Stroudsburg, PA 18360
USA
Tel: +1-570-476-8006
Fax: +1-570-476-0860
acl@aclweb.org

Introduction

Welcome to the Second Workshop on Bridging Human–Computer Interaction and Natural Language Processing!
The rapid advancement of natural language processing (NLP) research has led to a variety of applications spanning a wide range of domains. As NLP applications are being used by more people in their everyday lives, and are increasingly powered by data generated by people, it is more important than ever that NLP researchers and practitioners adopt and develop methods to incorporate people into their work in meaningful ways. Perspectives from human–computer interaction (HCI) can enable NLP researchers and practitioners to advance the field of NLP in ways that are aligned with people's needs, raising novel questions and research directions for both NLP and HCI.
The workshop brings together researchers and practitioners from both disciplines to discuss shared research interests, highlight work at the intersection of these fields, and identify challenges and opportunities for productive interdisciplinary collaborations.
We are delighted to present seventeen papers spanning reports of empirical work, research proposals, provocations, and surveys, of which eight are archival papers, and nine are non-archival papers to be presented at the workshop but not included in the proceedings.
We would like to thank everyone who submitted their work to this workshop, as well as the program committee for their insightful feedback. We would also like to thank our invited speakers: Jeffrey Bigham and Diyi Yang.
We hope you enjoy the workshop! —Su Lin Blodgett, Hal Daumé III, Michael Madaio, Ani Nenkova, Brendan O'Connor, Hanna Wallach, and Qian Yang

Organizing Committee

Organizers

Su Lin Blodgett, Microsoft Research
Hal Daumé III, Microsoft Research and University of Maryland
Michael Madaio, Microsoft Research
Ani Nenkova, Adobe Research
Brendan O'Connor, University of Massachusetts Amherst
Hanna Wallach, Microsoft Research
Qian Yang, Cornell University

Program Committee

Program Committee

Özge Alaçam, Bielefeld University
Michael S. Bernstein, Stanford University
Lawrence Birnbaum, Northwestern University
Heloisa Candello, IBM TJ Watson Research Center
Stevie Chancellor, University of Minnesota - Twin Cities
Leon Derczynski, IT University
Mitchell L. Gordon, Stanford University
Andrew Head, University of Pennsylvania
Hendrik Heuer, Universität Bremen
Matt Huenerfauth, Rochester Institute of Technology
Nanna Inie, IT University of Copenhagen
Maurice Jakesch, Cornell University
Mahmood Jasim, University of Massachusetts Amherst
Huda Khayrallah, Microsoft
Geza Kovacs, Lilt Inc.
Nikhil Krishnaswamy, Colorado State University
Alyssa Lees, Google
Nina Markl, Institute for Language, Cognition and Computation, University of Edinburgh
Marianna J. Martindale, University of Maryland, College Park
David Mimno, Cornell University
Swati Mishra, Cornell University
Tanu Mitra, University of Washington
Tatiana Passali, CERTH/ITI
Koustuv Saha, Georgia Institute of Technology
Joseph Seering, Stanford University
Indira Sen, GESIS
Qinlan Shen, Carnegie Mellon University
Weiyan Shi, Columbia University
Alison Smith-Renner, Dataminr
Soroush Vosoughi, Dartmouth College
Zijie J. Wang, Georgia Institute of Technology
Austin P. Wright, Georgia Institute of Technology
Ziyu Yao, George Mason University
Michael Miller Yoder, Carnegie Mellon University

Invited Speakers

Jeff Bigham, Carnegie Mellon University
Diyi Yang, Georgia Institute of Technology

Table of Contents

Program

Friday, July 15, 2022

08:30 - 08:35	*Day-1 Welcome + Opening Remarks*
08:35 - 09:30	*Day-1 Keynote 1*
09:30 - 10:00	*Day-1 Panel 1*
10:00 - 10:30	*Day-1 Break*
10:30 - 11:20	*Day-1 Panel 2*
11:20 - 12:00	*Day-1 Breakout discussion 1*
12:00 - 13:30	*Day-1 Lunch*
13:30 - 14:00	*Day-1 Panel 3*
14:00 - 14:40	*Day-1 Panel 4*
14:40 - 15:00	*Day-1 Panel 5*
15:00 - 15:30	*Day-1 Break*
15:30 - 16:30	*Day-1 Keynote 2*
16:30 - 16:55	*Day-1 Breakout discussion 2*
16:55 - 17:00	*Day-1 Closing Remarks*

Taxonomy Builder: a Data-driven and User-centric Tool for Streamlining Taxonomy Construction

John Hungerford[*], **Yee Seng Chan**[†], **Jessica MacBride**[†], **Benjamin M. Gyori**[‡], **Andrew Zupon**[◁], **Zheng Tang**[◁], **Egoitz Laparra**[◁], **Haoling Qiu**[†], **Bonan Min**[†], **Yan Zverev**[*], **Caitlin Hilverman**[⊕], **Max Thomas**[⊕], **Walt Andrews**[⊕], **Keith Alcock**[◁], **Zeyu Zhang**[◁], **Michael Reynolds**[*], **Mihai Surdeanu**[◁], **Steve Bethard**[◁], **Rebecca Sharp**[♠]

[*]Two Six Technologies, Arlington, VA, USA [†]Raytheon BBN Technologies, Cambridge, MA, USA
[‡]Harvard Medical School, Boston, MA, USA [◁]University of Arizona, Tucson, AZ, USA
[⊕]Qntfy, Arlington, VA, USA [♠]Lex Machina, Menlo Park, CA, USA
john.hungerford@twosixtech.com, msurdeanu@arizona.edu

Abstract

An existing domain taxonomy for normalizing content is often assumed when discussing approaches to information extraction, yet often in real-world scenarios there is none. When one does exist, as the information needs shift, it must be continually extended. This is a slow and tedious task, and one that does not scale well. Here we propose an interactive tool that allows a taxonomy to be built or extended *rapidly* and with a *human in the loop* to control precision. We apply insights from text summarization and information extraction to reduce the search space dramatically, then leverage modern pretrained language models to perform contextualized clustering of the remaining concepts to yield candidate nodes for the user to review. We show this allows a user to consider as many as 200 taxonomy concept candidates an hour to quickly build or extend a taxonomy to better fit information needs.

1 Introduction

Information extraction (IE), or the extraction of structured information from free text, is a sub-field of natural language processing (NLP) that is of keen interest to those outside of the NLP community. Practitioners who desire to mine information from text often set this up as a two-part task: (1) extracting the structured information from each document, and then (2) normalizing the extractions to be able to aggregate across a given corpus.

For this second step, often referred to as *grounding*, there are several approaches, but in industry and many domain-specific applications, the standard method for grounding is linking to a relevant ontology or taxonomy (Friedman et al., 2001; Srinivasan et al., 2002; Shen et al., 2014; Sevgili et al., 2020), i.e., a set of domain concepts and their hierarchical organization (and additional relations in the case of an ontology). However, the task of creating or maintaining these resources is laborious and never complete; as new documents are added or the use case shifts, there are concepts that are not well covered by the current taxonomy. As a result, typically a user must manually add new, relevant concepts to the taxonomy – a process which is both time-consuming and expensive.

Here we present a tool that is designed to streamline this process by using automatically gleaned text summarization analytics from the corpus itself, coupled with the power and expressivity of recent contextualized embeddings, to suggest candidate concepts to a human user during an interactive session. The user can accept, reject, or manipulate the suggested concept, then determine where it belongs in relation to other existing nodes. Taxonomies can be persisted for downstream use or a subsequent editing session. Our contributions are:

(1) We propose a data-driven approach to interactively build or augment a taxonomy with new concepts derived from the corpus of interest. The human user is at the center of our workflow and retains full control. Our approach first ranks and then clusters corpus concepts to provide the user with highly salient and coherent suggestions for new taxonomy nodes. In a web application, the user can act on the suggestions by adding, editing, deleting, or skipping them as desired. The tool is designed to be domain agnostic and interactive, with expensive steps performed in advance.

(2) We provide two case studies to demonstrate the utility of our approach, first, focused on a causal analysis of the drivers of food insecurity, and second, managing regional security (Section 5). We show that a user was able to process an average of 200 nodes per hour, 16% of which were added to the taxonomy. We find that the extended taxonomy results in an overall consistently higher grounding

Proceedings of the Second Workshop on Bridging Human–Computer Interaction and Natural Language Processing, pages 1 - 10
July 15, 2022 ©2022 Association for Computational Linguistics

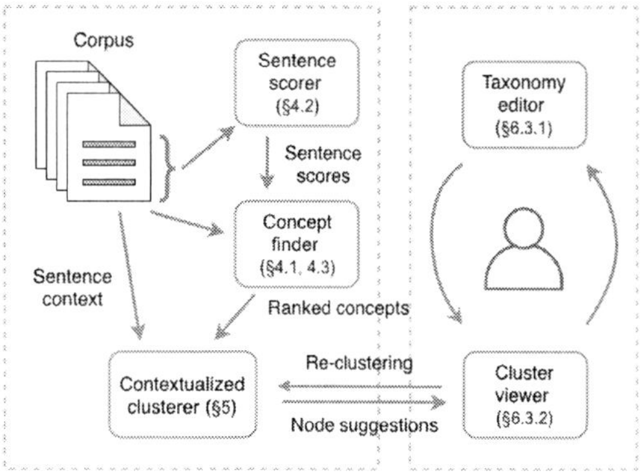

Figure 1: Overall architecture of our Taxonomy Builder, which combines offline pre-processing steps (the components in the left panel) with online user sessions (right panel).

confidence. We show that this increased confidence correlates with an increase in grounding correctness. Further, the updated taxonomy results in an increase in the number of causal relations between high-confidence grounded concepts.

2 Related work

There are several large, ontological resources, e.g., WordNet (Miller, 1995; Fellbaum, 2010), Cyc (Lenat, 1995), UMLS (Bodenreider, 2004), and SNOMED CT (Donnelly et al., 2006). However, resources such as these, even in aggregate, do not have coverage of all domains; instead, they need to be perpetually extended to cover new concepts (Powell et al., 2002; Ceusters, 2011).

To address the human cost of creating or maintaining taxonomies, many proposed approaches either rely on supervised data (Bordea et al., 2016; Mao et al., 2018; Espinosa-Anke et al., 2016, e.g.,) or perform unsupervised term extraction and clustering (Bisson et al., 2000; Drymonas et al., 2010, e.g.,). As supervised training cannot be assumed in real-world settings, our approach is more similar to the latter; we use unsupervised methods for concept discovery, ranking, and clustering. However, we keep the human in the loop to guide the process, critical for sensitive use cases such as military events, medical emergencies, etc.

Maedche and Staab (2001) similarly propose a tool that allows a user to guide a semi-automatic ontology creation process. However, our approach uses techniques from text summarization to filter candidate concepts and modern contextualized embeddings to more robustly handle multiple word senses and multi-word phrases to minimize the work that must be done by the user.

3 Architecture

Our approach for rapid data-driven taxonomy generation combines insights from several layers of text understanding to suggest highly relevant candidate concepts to a user, who decides how to use them (or not) to build the taxonomy they need. The architecture is shown in Figure 1.

Specifically, given a corpus of documents and optionally an existing taxonomy, we assign salience scores to each sentence based on keyword occurrence (Appendix A.1). From sentences with a sufficiently high salience, we extract multi-word expressions (noun and verb phrases) as potential phrases of interest. These are ranked with respect to each other using an extension of the TextRank algorithm (Mihalcea and Tarau, 2004) (Appendix A.3). The top-ranked concepts are encoded with contextualized word embeddings and clustered (Appendix B). Resulting clusters are presented to the user as suggested novel concepts; the phrases in the clusters can be thought of as *examples* of that concept. To ensure interactivity, these computationally expensive steps are done ahead of time, and the user need only load the pre-computed initial clusters.

Once loaded, clusters are exposed to the user through our interactive web application. The user can then decide between a series of actions (Section 4); specifically, they can *accept*, *edit*, *skip*, or *discard* the node. Accepted nodes are then inserted into the current working taxonomy. The user continues to work through the system's suggestions until they are satisfied with the taxonomy.

4 Taxonomy builder workflow

Once phrases are ranked and clustered, they are passed to the user-facing interface, which implements a two-part workflow: (a) cluster curation and (b) concept organization.

4.1 Cluster curation workflow

We frame the **cluster curation** workflow as a potentially iterative process, where the user adds novel nodes to the taxonomy from the suggested clusters and then, if desired, submits unused phrases for reclustering and a subsequent iteration of curation. By eliminating phrases that are irrelevant or have already been associated with a taxonomy node, each iteration provides an improved basis for organizing the remaining phrases into new, potentially usable clusters. The workflow for a curation iteration is illustrated in Figure 2:

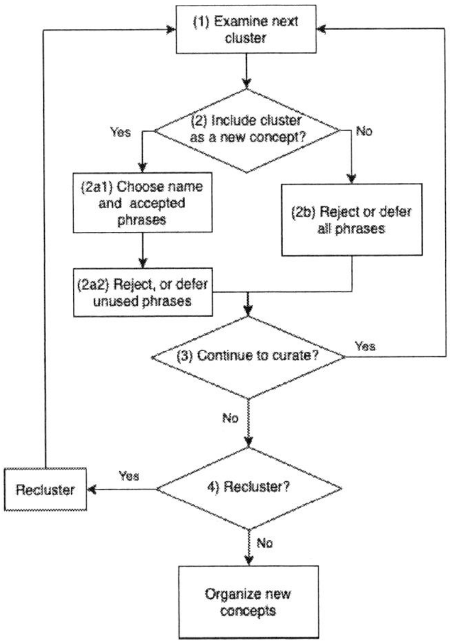

Figure 2: Cluster curation workflow.

1 User examines clusters in descending order of cluster score.

2 For each cluster, the user decides whether to include it as a taxonomy node, informed by its perceived relevance to the use case and its perceived added value, relative to existing nodes.

2a1 If the cluster is included, one phrase is selected for the node *name* and one or more phrases are chosen as concept *examples*; this can be done in bulk.

2a2 User can also *reject* or *defer* unused phrases from this cluster. Rejected phrases are excluded from reclustering, whereas deferred phrases are included if the user chooses to recluster.

2b If the cluster is not included in (2), the user can either reject or defer the entire cluster, or some of its phrases.

3 User decides whether to continue to curate or, if remaining clusters appear to be unlikely candidates for inclusion, to *defer* the remaining clusters.

4 Having completed an iteration of curation, the user either reclusters or moves on to the concept organization workflow.

4.2 Concept organization workflow

The **concept organization** workflow is: Examining each of the newly generated concepts in turn, the user 1) searches for an existing taxonomy node that would be a suitable parent to the new concept, 2) adds the concept to an existing branch if one is found or a new branch if none exists, and 3) updates any additional required concept metadata. Once all concepts have been organized within the taxonomy, the user publishes the new or augmented taxonomy.

4.3 User interface

The above workflows are carried out using a web application that includes a cluster viewer and a taxonomy editor. The **cluster viewer** displays the clustered concepts and allows the user to include or exclude clusters. The **taxonomy editor** allows the user to traverse the taxonomy tree, add or remove nodes, move existing nodes to different branches, and make changes to node metadata. The user can toggle between these at any time.

4.3.1 Cluster viewer

The cluster viewer consists of 1) reclustering controls, 2) a cluster list, and 3) a target node editor. The reclustering controls allow the user to submit new clustering jobs and access previously submitted jobs. The cluster list displays all clusters in descending order of score and contains controls for adding clusters to the taxonomy as concept nodes. The target node editor permits directly editing a new or existing taxonomy node corresponding to the given cluster (see Figure 3).

Each displayed cluster has a panel showing a) a node selector tool allowing a user to select an existing node or create a new node in the taxonomy as the "target" for the current cluster, b) a recommended concept name, initially populated by the first phrase within the cluster, c) a switch to either reject or curate the cluster (*curate* by default), d) the list of cluster phrases, e) phrases selected for inclusion, f) rejected phrases. Each cluster phrase has an option to *accept* it as an example, *reject* it, or *select it as the concept name*. The target node can be updated in the target node editor panel (3) and even moved in the taxonomy by updating its "parent" field. Through the inclusion of defaults, we ensure that the user does not need to treat all phrases, saving them time.

When the user first enters the cluster viewer, the application fetches and displays the initial clustering results. Once the user has included at least one cluster as a new concept by accepting a phrase, the option to recluster is enabled. When the user executes this option, the application submits a clustering job including all deferred phrases, clears the cluster results, and polls the clustering service for the job status. When the new clustering job is finished, the new cluster results are displayed and the job id is persisted in the application state for that user, allowing the user to follow the curation workflow over multiple iterations despite interruptions. Accepted clusters are automatically added to a top-level branch in the taxonomy named "clusters." Any changes to a cluster's name and accepted phrases automatically propagate to the

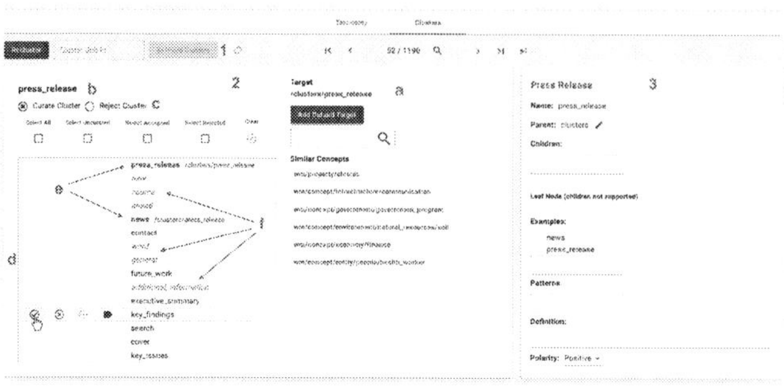

Figure 3: Cluster viewer user interface. Number and letter labels refer to the elements as described in Section 4.3.1.

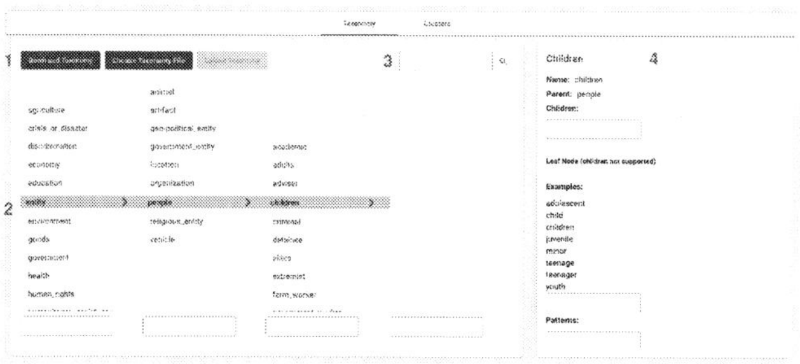

Figure 4: Taxonomy editor user interface. Number labels refer to the elements as described in Section 4.3.2.

corresponding concept's name and examples.

4.3.2 Taxonomy editor

The taxonomy editor consists of 1) import/export controls, 2) taxonomy explorer, 3) concept search widget, and 4) node editor (Figure 4). The import/export controls permit the user to upload a taxonomy and download the current state of a taxonomy as a taxonomy file. The taxonomy explorer provides a collapsed tree view of the taxonomy similar to multi-directory views common to many operating systems. This permits users to see a selected node, its siblings, its children, and its closest three ancestors and their siblings. Visible nodes can be clicked to become the new selection, allowing users to traverse the taxonomy in any "direction." This format was chosen because it displays a relatively broad cross-section of the taxonomy without sacrificing intelligibility and navigability. The concept search widget allows users to search for concept names and navigate to them without having to click through the explorer. The node editor allows users to update the concept name, update its parent, add and remove children, and update node metadata.

5 Usage Scenarios

We evaluate our tool through two use cases, both of which are motivated by DARPA's World Modelers program:[1] food insecurity and regional security. We detail both evaluations in Appendix C. The take-home messages from this evaluation were: (a) the users were able to process 200 candidates for taxonomy concepts per hour using the tool; (b) the updated taxonomies yielded increased grounding confidence scores, which indicate that the new taxonomies fit the data better, and (c) the new grounding confidence scores have increased correlation with grounding correctness.

6 Conclusions

We introduced a tool to streamline taxonomy construction and extension. Using techniques from text summarization alongside the benefits of modern pretrained language models, we automatically glean cohesive taxonomy node suggestions from the corpus itself. The user interface then allows users to quickly review suggestions and decide whether to accept or reject part or all of each. Through two case studies, we showed that this tool can be used to rapidly extend an existing taxonomy in a matter of hours, and further that the resulting taxonomy is a better fit to the domain of interest.

The software is included in the DART framework at: `https://github.com/twosixlabs-dart/dart-ui`.

[1] `https://www.darpa.mil/program/world-modelers`

References

Mehdi Allahyari, Seyedamin Pouriyeh, Mehdi Assefi, Saeid Safaei, Elizabeth D Trippe, Juan B Gutierrez, and Krys Kochut. 2017. Text summarization techniques: a brief survey. *arXiv preprint arXiv:1707.02268*.

Gilles Bisson, Claire Nédellec, and Dolores Canamero. 2000. Designing clustering methods for ontology building-the mo'k workbench. In *ECAI workshop on ontology learning*, volume 31. Citeseer.

Olivier Bodenreider. 2004. The unified medical language system (umls): integrating biomedical terminology. *Nucleic acids research*, 32(suppl_1):D267–D270.

Georgeta Bordea, Els Lefever, and Paul Buitelaar. 2016. SemEval-2016 task 13: Taxonomy extraction evaluation (TExEval-2). In *Proceedings of the 10th International Workshop on Semantic Evaluation (SemEval-2016)*, pages 1081–1091, San Diego, California. Association for Computational Linguistics.

Werner Ceusters. 2011. Snomed ct revisions and coded data repositories: when to upgrade? In *AMIA Annual Symposium Proceedings*, volume 2011, page 197. American Medical Informatics Association.

Kevin Donnelly et al. 2006. Snomed-ct: The advanced terminology and coding system for ehealth. *Studies in health technology and informatics*, 121:279.

Euthymios Drymonas, Kalliopi Zervanou, and Euripides G. M. Petrakis. 2010. Unsupervised ontology acquisition from plain texts: The ontogain system. In *Natural Language Processing and Information Systems*, pages 277–287, Berlin, Heidelberg. Springer Berlin Heidelberg.

Luis Espinosa-Anke, Horacio Saggion, Francesco Ronzano, and Roberto Navigli. 2016. Extasem! extending, taxonomizing and semantifying domain terminologies. In *Proceedings of the AAAI Conference on Artificial Intelligence*, volume 30.

Christiane Fellbaum. 2010. Wordnet. In *Theory and applications of ontology: computer applications*, pages 231–243. Springer.

Carol Friedman, Hongfang Liu, Lyudmila Shagina, Stephen Johnson, and George Hripcsak. 2001. Evaluating the umls as a source of lexical knowledge for medical language processing. In *Proceedings of the AMIA Symposium*, page 189. American Medical Informatics Association.

Benjamin M Gyori, John A Bachman, Kartik Subramanian, Jeremy L Muhlich, Lucian Galescu, and Peter K Sorger. 2017. From word models to executable models of signaling networks using automated assembly. *Molecular systems biology*, 13(11):954.

Douglas B Lenat. 1995. Cyc: A large-scale investment in knowledge infrastructure. *Communications of the ACM*, 38(11):33–38.

Hans Peter Luhn. 1958. The automatic creation of literature abstracts. *IBM Journal of research and development*, 2(2):159–165.

Alexander Maedche and Steffen Staab. 2001. Ontology learning for the semantic web. *IEEE Intelligent systems*, 16(2):72–79.

Debanjan Mahata, John Kuriakose, Rajiv Ratn Shah, and Roger Zimmermann. 2018. Key2Vec: Automatic ranked keyphrase extraction from scientific articles using phrase embeddings. In *Proceedings of the 2018 Conference of the North American Chapter of the Association for Computational Linguistics: Human Language Technologies, Volume 2 (Short Papers)*, pages 634–639, New Orleans, Louisiana. Association for Computational Linguistics.

Christopher D. Manning, Mihai Surdeanu, John Bauer, Jenny Finkel, Steven J. Bethard, and David McClosky. 2014. The stanford corenlp natural language processing toolkit. In *Proceedings of the 52nd Annual Meeting of the Association for Computational Linguistics (ACL)*.

Yuning Mao, Xiang Ren, Jiaming Shen, Xiaotao Gu, and Jiawei Han. 2018. End-to-end reinforcement learning for automatic taxonomy induction. *arXiv preprint arXiv:1805.04044*.

Rada Mihalcea and Paul Tarau. 2004. Textrank: Bringing order into text. In *Proceedings of the 2004 conference on empirical methods in natural language processing*, pages 404–411.

George A Miller. 1995. Wordnet: a lexical database for english. *Communications of the ACM*, 38(11):39–41.

Lawrence Page, Sergey Brin, Rajeev Motwani, and Terry Winograd. 1999. The pagerank citation ranking: Bringing order to the web. Technical report, Stanford InfoLab.

Patrick Pantel and Dekang Lin. 2002. Discovering word senses from text. In *Proceedings of the eighth ACM SIGKDD international conference on Knowledge discovery and data mining (SIGKDD-02)*, pages 613–619.

Jeffrey Pennington, Richard Socher, and Christopher D. Manning. 2014. Glove: Global vectors for word representation. In *Empirical Methods in Natural Language Processing (EMNLP)*, pages 1532–1543.

Tammy Powell, Suresh Srinivasan, Stuart J Nelson, William T Hole, Laura Roth, and Vladimir Olenichev. 2002. Tracking meaning over time in the umls metathesaurus. In *Proceedings of the AMIA Symposium*, page 622. American Medical Informatics Association.

Victor Sanh, Lysandre Debut, Julien Chaumond, and Thomas Wolf. 2020. Distilbert, a distilled version of bert: smaller, faster, cheaper and lighter.

Hinrich Schütze, Christopher D Manning, and Prabhakar Raghavan. 2008. *Introduction to information retrieval*, volume 39. Cambridge University Press Cambridge.

Ozge Sevgili, Artem Shelmanov, Mikhail Arkhipov, Alexander Panchenko, and Chris Biemann. 2020. Neural entity linking: A survey of models based on deep learning. *arXiv preprint arXiv:2006.00575*.

Rebecca Sharp, Adarsh Pyarelal, Benjamin Gyori, Keith Alcock, Egoitz Laparra, Marco A Valenzuela-Escárcega, Ajay Nagesh, Vikas Yadav, John Bachman, Zheng Tang, et al. 2019. Eidos, INDRA, & Delphi: From free text to executable causal models. In *Proceedings of the 2019 Conference of the North American Chapter of the Association for Computational Linguistics (Demonstrations)*.

Wei Shen, Jianyong Wang, and Jiawei Han. 2014. Entity linking with a knowledge base: Issues, techniques, and solutions. *IEEE Transactions on Knowledge and Data Engineering*, 27(2):443–460.

Suresh Srinivasan, Thomas C Rindflesch, William T Hole, Alan R Aronson, and James G Mork. 2002. Finding umls metathesaurus concepts in medline. In *Proceedings of the AMIA Symposium*, page 727. American Medical Informatics Association.

Thomas Wolf, Lysandre Debut, Victor Sanh, Julien Chaumond, Clement Delangue, Anthony Moi, Pierric Cistac, Tim Rault, Remi Louf, Morgan Funtowicz, Joe Davison, Sam Shleifer, Patrick von Platen, Clara Ma, Yacine Jernite, Julien Plu, Canwen Xu, Teven Le Scao, Sylvain Gugger, Mariama Drame, Quentin Lhoest, and Alexander Rush. 2020. Transformers: State-of-the-art natural language processing. In *Proceedings of the 2020 Conference on Empirical Methods in Natural Language Processing: System Demonstrations*, pages 38–45, Online. Association for Computational Linguistics.

A Concepts

For the process of selecting phrases from the corpus to serve as potential concepts of interest (or examples of those concepts), we use filters to both improve the speed of clustering and reduce the noise in the final clusters themselves.

A.1 Sentence salience

To prevent candidate phrases that are not salient to the core content of the documents, we use a simple *extractive text summarization* technique to identify the most salient or important sentences and assign each a score (Luhn, 1958; Allahyari et al., 2017).

We first lowercase document text and tokenize with `spaCy`,[2] ignoring stopwords and punctuation. We then extract keywords by calculating the frequency of all words, normalizing such that the most frequent has a value of 1. Finally, we calculate sentence salience scores by identifying the occurrence of keywords within a sentence, summing their frequency values, and normalizing these sums such that the most salient sentence in a document, i.e., the one with the highest sum, has a score of 1.

The sentence salience score quality was evaluated against a human rater. We selected random pairs of sentences, and for each asked our rater to determine which sentence was more important to the meaning of the document. A preliminary analysis with 10 news articles found that the human judgment agreed with the assigned scores 80% of the time. In cases of disagreement, typically the human chose a headline or summary sentence, whereas the algorithm chose a sentence with detailed but relevant information. From this preliminary analysis, we made two minor changes that made the model more robust to irregularities in documents: disregarding bullet points and subheadings. After making this change, rater judgments were nearly 100% aligned with the assigned salience scores.

A.2 Candidate phrases

To get candidate phrases from the sufficiently salient sentences, we process them with the CLU lab processors library.[3] We then select noun and verb chunks, splitting on coordinating conjunctions and trimming determiners from the edges. We note frequency and where they occur, keeping the 10k most frequent.

[2]`https://spacy.io`

[3]`https://github.com/clulab/processors` We use FastNLPProcessor, based on CoreNLP (Manning et al., 2014).

	Strategy 1	Strategy 2	Strategy 3
Expert 1	55%	30%	25%
Expert 2	70%	45%	25%

Table 1: Manual evaluation results (P@20) for three different strategies (Section A.3) for edge weights in the phrase graph. Strategy 1 uses $similarity$ alone, Strategy 2 uses $similarity \times PMI$, and Strategy 3 uses $similarity \times PMI \times frequency$. P@20 indicates what percentage of the concepts ranked in the top 20 were considered relevant for the use case by the corresponding expert.

A.3 Ranking candidates

These 10k phrases are ranked using an extension of TextRank (Mihalcea and Tarau, 2004), an algorithm inspired by PageRank (Page et al., 1999) that treats text as a graph and applies a graph-based ranking algorithm to surface keywords or phrases. The key extension in this effort is that nodes in the constructed graph are the phrases previously extracted, rather than full sentences, as in the original algorithm.

The algorithm consists of four steps: (1) Identify text units that best fit the task to be nodes in the graph; (2) Identify relations between units and draw the corresponding edges; (3) Iterate the graph-based ranking algorithm until convergence; (4) Sort nodes based on ranking scores.

As mentioned, in our implementation of TextRank, we consider our extracted chunks to be the text units (i.e., nodes in the graph) rather than complete sentences. We experimented with several options for defining edge weights, including word embedding similarity, Point-wise Mutual Information (PMI), and frequency of co-occurrence in the same sentence. (Mahata et al., 2018). For the embedding similarity, we represent each phrase as its GloVe embedding (Pennington et al., 2014), averaging embeddings of multi-word expressions, and compare with cosine similarity. Building on these three information sources, we compared three edge similarity strategies:

$$strategy_1 = cosine\_similarity(c_1, c_2) \quad (1)$$

$$strategy_2 = strategy_1 \times PMI(c_1, c_2) \quad (2)$$

$$strategy_3 = strategy_2 \times log(cooccur(c_1, c_2)) \quad (3)$$

where c_1 and c_2 are the phrases to be compared.

Using a small set of documents, we had two domain experts do a blind evaluation of the top-ranked phrases produced by the different strategies. As shown in Table 1, strategy 1 produces the best TextRank overall,[4] and so was chosen. To avoid a

[4]Post-hoc analysis showed that strategy 2 prefers infre-

fully connected graph, which slows down the TextRank algorithm dramatically, we set a threshold for the similarity scores[5] and for each phrase, we keep only edges for the 100 most similar neighbors.

After ranking the extracted phrases, the highest-ranked 5k are used for generating the node suggestion clusters (Section B).

B Clustering

After extraction, phrases are clustered into semantically cohesive groups to serve as taxonomy node suggestions. We use Huggingface transformers (Wolf et al., 2020) to obtain contextualized DistilBERT (Sanh et al., 2020) embeddings of each occurrence of each phrase. We then use Annoy[6] to perform time-efficient nearest neighbor search over these embeddings. For each phrase, we obtain a ranked list (in terms of cosine similarity) of the top-k most similar phrases as input to the clustering.

To cluster the phrases, we employ an algorithm based on the CBC algorithm (Clustering By Committee) (Pantel and Lin, 2002), which uses average link agglomerative clustering (Schütze et al., 2008, Ch. 17) to recursively form cohesive clusters that are dissimilar to one another. For each cluster c that is formed, the algorithm assigns a score: $|c|\times$ avgsim(c), where $|c|$ is the number of members of c and avgsim(c) is the average pairwise cosine similarity between members. This score reflects a preference for larger and cohesive clusters. We then rank the clusters in decreasing order of their cluster scores, prioritizing the most effective and cohesive clusters to the user for selection and addition to the taxonomy.

C Usage Scenarios and Discussion

We evaluate our tool through two use cases, both of which are motivated by DARPA's World Modelers program.[7] The first use case focuses on food insecurity, which is a complex domain, spanning several disciplines including economics, government policy, agriculture, etc. The second use case addresses regional security, an equally complex domain.

quent phrases that aren't descriptive of the overall topic, e.g., *intergovernmental panel* and *environ*, whereas strategy 3 oppositely adds frequent phrases, e.g., names of countries, which the experts deemed not useful for taxonomy construction.

[5]We found 0.0 to be both a useful and intuitive threshold.

[6]`https://github.com/spotify/annoy`

[7]`https://www.darpa.mil/program/world-modelers`

C.1 Use case 1: food insecurity

For this use case, the user[8] was provided with an initial taxonomy[9] created for the DARPA World Modelers program, and used the tool to perform cluster curation and taxonomy editing for 2 hours. In this time, the user was able to curate 400 clusters. Of those 400, 65 were chosen for inclusion as taxonomy nodes, 18 were *deferred* for reclustering, and the remaining 317 were *rejected* entirely. After this curation, the resulting taxonomy was compared against the original.

For this case study, we use a corpus of 472 documents from the food insecurity domain (government and NGO reports, news articles, etc.). We perform IE using the Eidos causal information extraction system (Sharp et al., 2019), resulting in 209,352 extracted concepts related to food security.

We then attempt to ground each concept mention to the taxonomy, assigning a grounding confidence score. There are many ways of assigning a confidence score. Here, we create a vector representation for the mention to be grounded and of each node in the taxonomy by averaging the GloVe embeddings for each non-stop word in the mention's text span and the taxonomy node's examples, respectively. We then assign each mention to the node that is closest in terms of cosine similarity.

We analyze extracted mentions and their grounding before and after the taxonomy update. Of the $209,352$ concepts extracted, $170,488$ were grounded before the update and $170,539$ were grounded after.[10] Further, after the update, $48,404$ concepts (28% of grounded concepts), were grounded to a different taxonomy term. For example, the phrase *ethnic-religious divisions* was originally grounded to the taxonomy concept `crisis_or_disaster/conflict/hostility` (with a score of 0.48), but after the update, it is grounded to `ethnic_conflicts` (with a higher score of 0.56).

Of the groundings that changed, for $47,518$ the confidence increased after the taxonomy update (98% of those that changed). Figure 5 shows the distribution of the changes in grounding scores attributed to the taxonomy update. Importantly, we observed that this increase in grounding confi-

[8]One of the authors served as the tool's user.

[9]`https://github.com/WorldModelers/Ontologies`

[10]The Eidos system has an internal filter that doesn't produce groundings when the confidence is below 0.2.

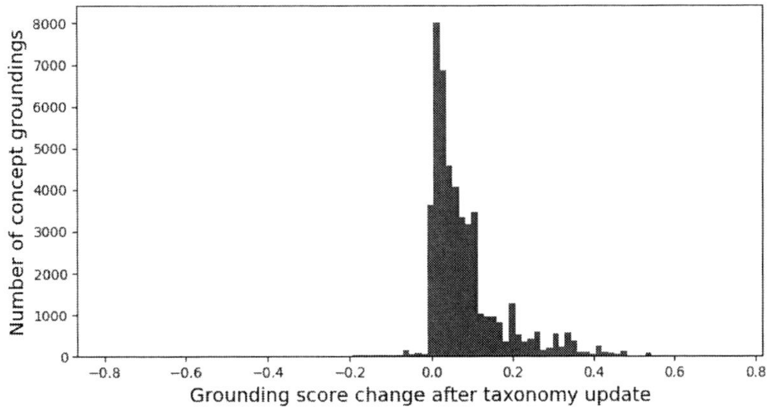

Figure 5: Histogram of changes in grounding scores associated with specific concepts after the taxonomy update in use case 1.

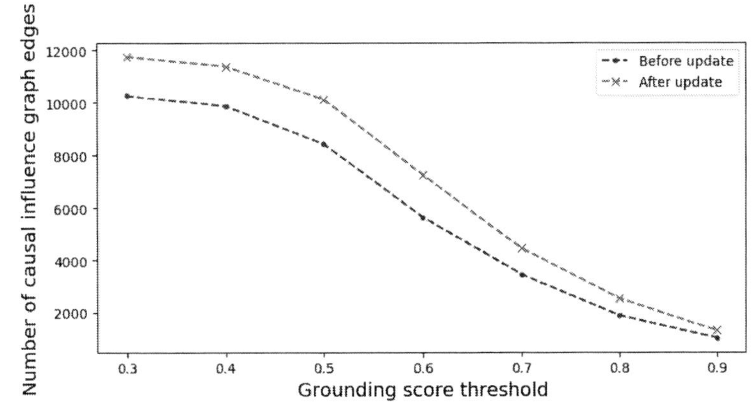

Figure 6: The number of causal influence graph edges over concepts obtained before and after the taxonomy update at a given grounding score threshold in use case 1.

dence correlates with grounding correctness. To verify this, we measured the Pearson correlation between grounding confidence and correctness (which is represented as a Boolean variable, i.e., correct/incorrect grounding) for 42 randomly selected concepts. The Pearson correlation values were 55.15% for the original taxonomy vs. 59.37% for the updated one, a relative increase of 7.6%.

Next, we use INDRA (Gyori et al., 2017; Sharp et al., 2019), an automated model assembly system, to assemble each set of causal influence relations (before and after taxonomy updating) into a causal influence graph by aggregating relations with matching groundings. We find that the number of edges in the causal influence graph increased from $11,072$ to $12,720$ after the taxonomy update, and further, we show in Figure 6 the number of edges in each influence graph between nodes whose grounding scores are above a given threshold. As shown, after the taxonomy update, the influence graph is consistently larger and covers more taxonomy terms compared to before, with higher confidence.

C.2 Use case 2: regional security

This use case was performed by a group of expert analysts outside the tool's developer team as part of a DARPA program evaluation. The analysis attempted to model a complex regional crisis scenario, using IE from documents to construct models of causal influences of security concerns surrounding Kenya's 2022 elections.

Users started from an initial taxonomy[11]. 10k documents relevant for the use case were identified by the organizers of the evaluation to seed the taxonomy extension process. Users were then given access to the tool to perform cluster curation and

[11] `https://github.com/WorldModelers/Ontologies`

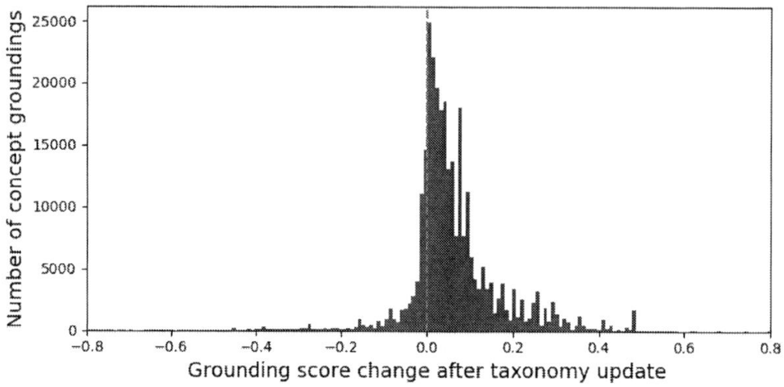

Figure 7: Histogram of changes in grounding scores associated with specific concepts after the taxonomy update in use case 2 (the red line provides vertical axis at 0 score change for clarity).

taxonomy editing over the course of multiple days.

Similar to use case 1, to evaluate the effect of taxonomy changes, we performed IE using Eidos on the seed corpus. This resulted in a total of $1,205,628$ concepts extracted from the 10k document corpus. We then grounded each extracted concept – using the approach described for use case 1 – with respect to the taxonomy both before and after the update. We found that $297,405$ of the extracted concepts (24.6% of all extracted) were grounded to different taxonomy entries after the update. Of these, $247,113$ (83%) were grounded with a higher score compared to before (see Figure 7 for the distribution of score changes).

Using INDRA, we then assembled causal relations that were extracted between concepts from the corpus into a causal influence graph before and after the taxonomy update. In both cases, we applied a grounding score threshold of 0.6 to retain concepts grounded to a taxonomy term with high-confidence. We found that the number of nodes in the graph increased from 337 to 451 (an increase of 33.8%) and the number of edges grew from $23,274$ to $29,562$ (a 27.6% increase) after the update. Overall, we again found that the taxonomy update resulted in a larger causal influence graph at a given level of confidence.

An Interactive Exploratory Tool for the Task of Hate Speech Detection

Angelina McMillan-Major[1,3] and **Amandalynne Paullada**[2] and **Yacine Jernite**[3]
Department of Linguistics, University of Washington, Seattle, USA[1]
Department of Biomedical Informatics & Medical Education, University of Washington, Seattle, USA[2]
Hugging Face[3]
aymm@uw.edu, paullada@uw.edu, yacine@huggingface.co

Abstract

With the growth of Automatic Content Moderation (ACM) on widely used social media platforms, transparency into the design of moderation technology and policy is necessary for online communities to advocate for themselves when harms occur. In this work, we describe a suite of interactive modules to support the exploration of various aspects of this technology, and particularly of those components that rely on English models and datasets for hate speech detection, a subtask within ACM. We intend for this demo to support the various stakeholders of ACM in investigating the definitions and decisions that underpin current technologies such that those with technical knowledge and those with contextual knowledge may both better understand existing systems.

1 Introduction

The field of natural language processing (NLP) is organized into *tasks*, definitions of which minimally include the combination of a modeling paradigm and benchmark datasets (Vu et al. (2020); Reuver et al. (2021); Schlangen (2021); see also BIG-bench[1]). This organization, however, is not necessarily apparent to those outside of NLP research. Making these established tasks outwardly visible is one step towards the recent push for accessible documentation of NLP (Bender and Friedman, 2018; Holland et al., 2018; Mitchell et al., 2019; Arnold et al., 2019; McMillan-Major et al., 2021; Gebru et al., 2021) and promoting the importance of careful data treatment (Paullada et al., 2021; Sambasivan et al., 2021b).

One task that has attracted sustained interest in NLP is the problem of content moderation. While many manual and hybrid paradigms for content moderation exist (Pershan, 2020), several major platforms have invested heavily in automated methods that they see as necessary to support scaling up moderation to address their colossal content loads (Gillespie, 2020). Automatic Content Moderation (ACM) includes strategies that range from keyword- or regular expression-based approaches, to hash-based content recognition, to data-driven machine learning models. These approaches employ different families of algorithms, resulting in various downstream effects and necessitating documentation and algorithmic accountability processes that address the needs of a variety of stakeholders.

Synchronizing research around consistent modeling paradigms and benchmark datasets is an ongoing problem for ACM (Fortuna et al., 2020; Madukwe et al., 2020), with experts calling for more grounding in related areas in the social sciences, communication studies and psychology (Vidgen and Derczynski, 2020; Kiritchenko et al., 2021). Without this grounding and without consideration for the contexts into which ACM is integrated, the technology intended to prevent harms ends up magnifying them, especially for vulnerable communities (Dias Oliva et al., 2021).

The present paper proposes an interactive tool aimed at allowing a diverse audience to explore examples of NLP data and models used in data-driven ACM, focusing on the subtask of hate speech detection. Our tool outlines various aspects of the social and technical considerations for ACM, provides an overview of the data and modeling landscape for hate speech detection, and enables comparison of different resources and approaches to the task. Our goal is to understand the role of multidisciplinary education and documentation in promoting algorithmic transparency and contestability (Vaccaro et al., 2019). We provide a brief overview of ACM as well as the interactions between its many stakeholders (§2) and describe related work in dataset and model exploration (§3). We then present our demo (§4), highlighting its constituent sections and describing our rationale for each. We conclude with a summary of limitations and future work (§5).

[1] https://github.com/google/BIG-bench/

Proceedings of the Second Workshop on Bridging Human–Computer Interaction and Natural Language Processing, pages 11 - 20
July 15, 2022 ©2022 Association for Computational Linguistics

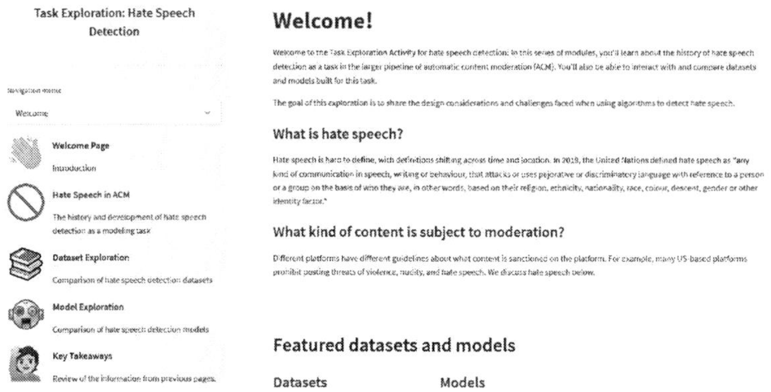

Figure 1: Introduction page to the demo

2 Background: Content Moderation

Content moderation is the process by which online platforms manage which kinds of content, in the form of images, video, or text, that users are allowed to share. Policies for content moderation, which vary across platforms, are often guided by a combination of legal, commercial, and social pressures. Broadly, these policies tend to prohibit explicit sexual content, graphic depictions of violence, hate speech[2], and harassment or trolling between platform users (Gillespie, 2018). Platforms take a variety of actions to moderate content, including removal of the offending content, reducing the visibility of the content, adding a flag or warning, and/or suspending accounts that violate content guidelines. Moderation decisions can, however, lead to undesired reactions. For example, removing conspiracy theory content tends to reinforce conspiracy theory claims, and ousting hateful groups from larger platforms can result in these groups flocking to smaller platforms with fewer resources for moderation (Pershan, 2020).

Conflicts in moderation decisions often arise due to the size and diversity of a platform's community members and a divergence in priorities between community members and platform managers. A report from the Brennan Center for Justice found that 'double standards' pervade in content moderation actions, and that inconsistently applied content policies overwhelmingly silence marginalized voices (Díaz and Hecht-Felella). For example, Facebook erroneously labeled hashtags referencing Al-Aqsa, a mosque in a predominately Palestinian neighborhood of Jerusalem, as pertaining to a terrorist organization, and was also found to censor derogatory speech against white people more frequently than slurs against Black, Jewish, and transgender people (Eidelman et al., 2021). To address the often stark gap between model performance on intrinsic metrics and performance in real-world, user-facing scenarios for toxic content classifiers, Gordon et al. (2021) propose an evaluation paradigm that takes into account inter-annotator disagreements on training data.

Even when moderation rules are applied consistently, they may result in over-moderating communities that use terms that are deemed 'explicit' outside the community but are acceptable to the community members themselves, as often happens for LGBTQ communities online (Dias Oliva et al., 2021). These kinds of harms show that content moderation algorithms must be developed with transparency, care for the context in which the algorithms will be integrated, and mechanisms for the community to contest moderation decisions. One approach to consulting diverse perspectives on 'toxic' content relies on *jury learning*, as in a model proposed by Gordon et al. (2022).

In addition to calling for more inclusion by various stakeholders in decision-making processes for each platform, Pershan (2020) advocates for the development of regional policies that consider the moderation styles of smaller platforms as well as larger ones. Regional policies are especially important as the large platforms, primarily located in the US, are ported outside the US with moderation policies that are ill-equipped to support local communities appropriately, for example in India where hate speech may also occur on the basis of caste (Sambasivan et al., 2021a).

Approaches to content moderation commonly involve a hybrid strategy that uses reports from users

[2] We define *hate speech* in §4.

and algorithmic systems to identify content that may violate platform guidelines, and then relies on human review to determine a course of action (i.e., retain, obscure, or remove the content). This process exposes human moderators to high volumes of violent and hateful content (Roberts, 2014), motivating a push for enhanced automatic methods to alleviate the burden on human moderators. Automated content moderation can rely on analyses of the content itself using NLP or computer vision (CV), features of user dynamics, and hashing to match instances of pre-identified forbidden content. Within the realm of text-based ACM, approaches vary from wordlist-based approaches to data-driven models. When platforms opt not to build their own systems, Perspective API[3] is commonly used to flag various kinds of content for moderation.

Forbidding hate speech on online platforms is seen as a way to prevent the proliferation of hateful discourse from leading to hate-driven violence offline[4]. Common datasets used for training and evaluating hate speech detectors can be found at `https://hatespeechdata.com/`. We refer readers to Kiritchenko et al. (2021) for a comprehensive overview of definitions, resources, and ethical challenges incurred in the development of hate speech detection technologies.

3 Related Work: Interactive Dataset and Model Exploration

A variety of methods and tools that enable dataset users to explore and familiarize themselves with the contents of the datasets have been proposed. For example, Know Your Data[5], provided by Google's PAIR research group, aims to provide users with views of datasets that surface errors or issues with particular instances, systematic gaps in representation, or problematic content that requires human judgment to assess. This tool thus far has focused on image datasets. The Dataset Cartography method, proposed by Swayamdipta et al. (2020), uses model training dynamics to create maps of dataset instances organized by difficulty or ambiguity, which can surface problematic instances. Recently, Xiao et al. (2022) released a tool for comparing datasets aimed at enabling dataset users to understand potential sources of bias in the data. While much previous work has focused on exploratory tools for dataset *users*, our tool is meant to cater to an audience who will not necessarily be training machine learning models, but constitute a variety of impacted or interested stakeholders.

Wright et al. (2021) tackle the problem of interrogating a toxicity detection model using a tool they call RECAST. They fine-tune a BERT-based Transformer model on the Jigsaw Kaggle dataset of toxic comments from Wikipedia and provide an online text-editing application that visually highlights words that the models detects as toxic, suggesting alternate phrases that may be less toxic using both word embeddings and language modeling predictions. They evaluate the tool using a text-editing task, presenting user study participants with comments drawn from both the Kaggle dataset and Twitter threads, and show that the users in their study are learning about the model behavior by editing toxic comments to be less toxic according to the model prediction scores.

4 Demo Development and Structure

We aim to make the exploration tool as accessible and useful as possible to the many stakeholders involved in ACM. Particularly in light of the closed nature of many contemporary content moderation pipelines that impact people who use social media, our demo familiarizes these stakeholders with the general framework of how such systems might work behind the scenes. In order to conceptualize the breadth of uses that ACM stakeholders may have for such an exploratory tool, we considered the stakeholders and their goals detailed in Pershan (2020) using the framework developed by Suresh et al. (2021). Rather than identifying stakeholders based on their roles, they propose mapping stakeholders based on the type of knowledge they hold and the context of that knowledge, such as technical, domain, and contextual knowledge.

In mapping out our envisioned stakeholders, we tried to consider how they might use the tool towards their goals. Policymakers, journalists and impacted communities may use the demo to understand where and how things go wrong in hate speech detection in order to advocate for changes to platform policies. Domain experts may use the tool to understand where their work is used in a pipeline, such as in label definitions, and envision potential locations in the pipeline where additional domain information could be useful. Students and current developers may use the tool to reflect upon

[3]`https://perspectiveapi.com/`
[4]Discord Off-Platform Behavior Update
[5]`https://knowyourdata.withgoogle.com/`

their own design decisions in light of the historical and sociotechnical framing we provide for ACM and consider new possibilities for research development. Finally, we imagine that our demo may generally provide common ground for these and other stakeholders in order to facilitate more productive discussions on how to develop ACM technologies.

Additionally, in order to more fully understand the perspectives of stakeholders outside of the academic context, we discussed our demo and the state of the field of hate speech detection with several experts in the field, particularly those with experience deploying models in the industry context and working with non-technical stakeholders. Following these discussions, we built the interactive, openly available demo using Streamlit[6], the first page of which is shown in Fig. 1. We provide screenshots of the other modules in Appendix A.

S1. Welcome and Introduction

The introduction to the demo is intended to provide common ground for the various stakeholders with key terms and the kinds of data that are subject to moderation. The key terms include *hate speech* and *content moderation*, for which we provide the following definitions to help build a shared understanding given the broad audience we identified:

Hate speech Any kind of communication in speech, writing, or behaviour that attacks or uses pejorative or discriminatory language with reference to a person or a group on the basis of who they are, in other words, based on their religion, ethnicity, nationality, race, colour, descent, gender or other identity factor (United Nations, 2019).

Content moderation A collection of interventions used by online platforms to partially obscure, or remove entirely from user-facing view, content that is objectionable based on the company's values or community guidelines.

Additionally, we provide a list of the datasets and models that we feature in the tool along with links to further documentation for each resource.

S2. Context of ACM

To contextualize automatic hate speech detection tools, we describe of the kinds of content that moderation is intended to target and how automatic methods are used to support manual approaches to content moderation, as discussed in §2 and §3. We also illustrate the ongoing challenges in hate speech detection with links to platforms' content guidelines and press releases in addition to critical works in response to content moderation.

S3. Hate Speech Dataset Exploration

Meaningfully exploring datasets composed of up to hundreds of thousands of instances constitutes a signifcant difficulty. To address this challenge, we rely on hierarchical clustering to group similar examples at different levels of granularity, using SentenceBERT (Reimers and Gurevych, 2019) embeddings of the example text to evaluate closeness. For each cluster (including the top-level one corresponding to the full dataset), the text of a selection of examplars for that cluster may be viewed along with their labels, as well as the distribution of labels within the entire cluster. This allows users of our system to zoom in on specific regions, and gain insights into what sorts of examples are represented in a dataset and how different topics are labeled. Comparison across datasets also illustrates the different assumptions that are made at the time of dataset creation even within the same established task. For this demo, we pre-selected datasets constructed for hate speech detection in English. These include the FRENK Dataset of Socially Unacceptable Discourse in English (Ljubešić et al., 2019), the Measuring Hate Speech dataset (Kennedy et al., 2020), and the Twitter Sentiment Analysis dataset (Sharma, 2019).

S4. Hate Speech Model Exploration

In the model exploration section, we provide two ways of probing models. The first allows viewers to submit one or more test inputs to a single model. The results are then shown such that viewers may select a label and order the output scores for the inputs based on that label. The second module compares the same input sentence with two different models. The module then returns the label and score given by each model as well as a confidence graphs for each model. The confidence graphs show the model's accuracy, errors, and scores over hateful and non-hateful instances as well as out-of-domain content from the Hateful Memes and Open Subtitles datasets (Kiela et al., 2020; Tiedemann, 2016). These graphs provide context for an individual instance of model behavior, showing whether the model is likely to be more or less confident when labeling an instance, regardless of the model's overall accuracy. Again,

[6]`https://streamlit.io/`

for the demo we pre-selected models including a RoBERTa model trained on the FRENK dataset (Ljubešić et al., 2019), a RoBERTa model trained on the TweetEval benchmark (Barbieri et al., 2020), and a DeHateBERT model trained on Twitter and StormFront data (Aluru et al., 2021).

To support viewers in probing the models, the demo also supplies test case instances from Röttger et al. (2021)'s HateCheck tests. The tests use templates to generate examples of text that are likely to mislabeled by hate speech detection models. The templates are organized into classes based on the linguistic properties of the sentence, such as whether it contains negation or counter speech, and have placeholders for social groups that are frequently targeted by hate speech. The counter speech template class, for example, contains sentences that directly reference or quote hate speech, as in "Statements like '[IDENTITY] are scum' are deeply hurtful." (examples from Röttger et al. (2021), p.45). These kinds of sentences are often labeled as hateful by automatic systems due to the direct reference, but the sentence as a whole provides context that shows that the intent is not hate speech. With 29 different groups of examples over 10 different classes in addition to counter speech, the HateCheck tests encourage users to think of the variety of forms that hate speech can take and how they may be misclassified by automatic systems.

While the single model exploration module is similar in function to the RECAST tool (Wright et al., 2021), we note significant differences in the imagined use cases of ours and the RECAST tool. Wright et al. emphasize RECAST's use in real time as a comment-editing tool. Our tool on the other hand is not intended for integrated use, but rather as a self-directed learning tool. While stakeholders could compare several edits of the same comment using our tool, stakeholders are not limited to this method of exploration. We instead encourage stakeholders to consider comparisons, between inputs and between models, as a way to surface expected and unexpected model behavior.

S5. Demo Feedback Questionnaire

To end the demo, we ask the user for feedback on their role and experience with the modules. The questions focus on what the user learned from the modules about the sociotechnical aspects of ACM and the resources for hate speech detection. In particular, we are interested in seeing how the modules were more or less informative for different stakeholder groups. See Appendix B for the specific questions asked.

5 Limitations and Future Work

While our tool is aimed at promoting a shared vocabulary and common ground between (1) those who build and design hate speech detection datasets and models, (2) those who are on the receiving end of moderation decisions on social media platforms, and (3) researchers and journalists who are interested in understanding some of the mechanics of automated content moderation, the tool is not designed to be a platform for facilitating connection and engagement *between* these groups. However, the tool can serve as a foundation for such discussions and could be integrated into a larger system designed for engagement.

We plan to update the demo based on feedback from the questionnaire. Once the demo has been finalized, user studies aimed at gathering perspectives from a broader set of stakeholders, including those we did not consider in our initial design process such as content moderation workers, would help to outline how different stakeholders actually use the tool and evaluate the effectiveness of the tool with respect to the participants' use cases and contexts. Following these studies, future versions of the tool could expand to consider more issues within content moderation beyond hate speech detection or be designed to provide context for other kinds of NLP tasks. While this current demo is focused on English resources, future versions could also include resources and contexts for other languages as well as more complex configurations of datasets and models beyond binary labeling schemas.

We began this work with the intention to help provide clarity into the organization of the field of NLP into various tasks. While this demo has focused on the task of ACM, we would expect that similar demos could be developed to contextualize other well-known tasks in NLP such as machine translation, information retrieval, and automatic speech recognition.

Acknowledgements

Thank you to Zeerak Talat, Dia Kayyali, Bertie Vidgen, and the Perspective API Team for their insightful comments during the development of the demo, and to the anonymous reviewers for their very thoughtful and helpful suggestions for improving this publication.

A.P. is supported by the National Institutes of Health, National Library of Medicine (NLM) Biomedical and Health Informatics Training Program at the University of Washington (Grant Nr. T15LM007442). The content is solely the responsibility of the authors and does not necessarily represent the official views of the National Institutes of Health.

References

Sai Saketh Aluru, Binny Mathew, Punyajoy Saha, and Animesh Mukherjee. 2021. A deep dive into multilingual hate speech classification. In *Machine Learning and Knowledge Discovery in Databases. Applied Data Science and Demo Track*, pages 423–439, Cham. Springer International Publishing.

Matthew Arnold, Rachel K. E. Bellamy, Michael Hind, Stephanie Houde, Sameep Mehta, Aleksandra Mojsilović, Ravi Nair, Karthikeyan Natesan Ramamurthy, Alexandra Olteanu, David Piorkowski, Darrell Reimer, John Richards, Jason Tsay, and Kush R. Varshney. 2019. Factsheets: Increasing trust in ai services through supplier's declarations of conformity. *IBM Journal of Research and Development*, 63(4/5):6:1–6:13.

Francesco Barbieri, Jose Camacho-Collados, Luis Espinosa Anke, and Leonardo Neves. 2020. TweetEval: Unified benchmark and comparative evaluation for tweet classification. In *Findings of the Association for Computational Linguistics: EMNLP 2020*, pages 1644–1650, Online. Association for Computational Linguistics.

Emily M. Bender and Batya Friedman. 2018. Data statements for natural language processing: Toward mitigating system bias and enabling better science. *Transactions of the Association for Computational Linguistics*, 6:587–604.

Thiago Dias Oliva, Dennys Marcelo Antonialli, and Alessandra Gomes. 2021. Fighting hate speech, silencing drag queens? artificial intelligence in content moderation and risks to lgbtq voices online. *Sexuality & Culture*, 25(2):700–732.

Ángel Díaz and Laura Hecht-Felella. Double standards in social media content moderation. *Brennan Center for Justice at New York University School of Law.*

Vera Eidelman, Adeline Lee, and Fikayo Walter-Johnson. 2021. Time and again, social media giants get content moderation wrong: Silencing speech about al-aqsa mosque is just the latest example. *American Civil Liberties Union.*

Paula Fortuna, Juan Soler, and Leo Wanner. 2020. Toxic, hateful, offensive or abusive? what are we really classifying? an empirical analysis of hate speech datasets. In *Proceedings of the 12th Language Resources and Evaluation Conference*, pages 6786–6794, Marseille, France. European Language Resources Association.

Timnit Gebru, Jamie Morgenstern, Briana Vecchione, Jennifer Wortman Vaughan, Hanna Wallach, Hal Daumé III, and Kate Crawford. 2021. Datasheets for datasets. *Commun. ACM*, 64(12):86–92.

Tarleton Gillespie. 2018. *Custodians of the Internet: Platforms, content moderation, and the hidden decisions that shape social media.* Yale University Press.

Tarleton Gillespie. 2020. Content moderation, ai, and the question of scale. *Big Data & Society*, 7(2):2053951720943234.

Mitchell L Gordon, Michelle S Lam, Joon Sung Park, Kayur Patel, Jeff Hancock, Tatsunori Hashimoto, and Michael S Bernstein. 2022. Jury learning: Integrating dissenting voices into machine learning models. In *CHI Conference on Human Factors in Computing Systems*, pages 1–19.

Mitchell L Gordon, Kaitlyn Zhou, Kayur Patel, Tatsunori Hashimoto, and Michael S Bernstein. 2021. The disagreement deconvolution: Bringing machine learning performance metrics in line with reality. In *Proceedings of the 2021 CHI Conference on Human Factors in Computing Systems*, pages 1–14.

Sarah Holland, Ahmed Hosny, Sarah Newman, Joshua Joseph, and Kasia Chmielinski. 2018. The dataset nutrition label: A framework to drive higher data quality standards.

Chris J. Kennedy, Geoff Bacon, Alexander Sahn, and Claudia von Vacano. 2020. Constructing interval variables via faceted rasch measurement and multitask deep learning: a hate speech application.

Douwe Kiela, Hamed Firooz, Aravind Mohan, Vedanuj Goswami, Amanpreet Singh, Pratik Ringshia, and Davide Testuggine. 2020. The hateful memes challenge: Detecting hate speech in multimodal memes.

Svetlana Kiritchenko, Isar Nejadgholi, and Kathleen C Fraser. 2021. Confronting abusive language online: A survey from the ethical and human rights perspective. *Journal of Artificial Intelligence Research*, 71:431–478.

Nikola Ljubešić, Darja Fišer, and Tomaž Erjavec. 2019. The frenk datasets of socially unacceptable discourse in slovene and english. In *Text, Speech, and Dialogue*, pages 103–114, Cham. Springer International Publishing.

Kosisochukwu Madukwe, Xiaoying Gao, and Bing Xue. 2020. In data we trust: A critical analysis of hate speech detection datasets. In *Proceedings of the Fourth Workshop on Online Abuse and Harms*, pages 150–161, Online. Association for Computational Linguistics.

Angelina McMillan-Major, Salomey Osei, Juan Diego Rodriguez, Pawan Sasanka Ammanamanchi, Sebastian Gehrmann, and Yacine Jernite. 2021. Reusable templates and guides for documenting datasets and models for natural language processing and generation: A case study of the HuggingFace and GEM data and model cards. In *Proceedings of the 1st Workshop on Natural Language Generation, Evaluation, and Metrics (GEM 2021)*, pages 121–135, Online. Association for Computational Linguistics.

Margaret Mitchell, Simone Wu, Andrew Zaldivar, Parker Barnes, Lucy Vasserman, Ben Hutchinson, Elena Spitzer, Inioluwa Deborah Raji, and Timnit Gebru. 2019. Model cards for model reporting. In *Proceedings of the Conference on Fairness, Accountability, and Transparency*, FAT* '19, page 220–229, New York, NY, USA. Association for Computing Machinery.

Amandalynne Paullada, Inioluwa Deborah Raji, Emily M Bender, Emily Denton, and Alex Hanna. 2021. Data and its (dis) contents: A survey of dataset development and use in machine learning research. *Patterns*, 2(11):100336.

Claire Pershan. 2020. Moderating our (dis)content: Renewing the regulatory approach. In *Proceedings of the Fourth Workshop on Online Abuse and Harms*, page 113, Online. Association for Computational Linguistics.

Nils Reimers and Iryna Gurevych. 2019. Sentence-bert: Sentence embeddings using siamese bert-networks. In *Proceedings of the 2019 Conference on Empirical Methods in Natural Language Processing and the 9th International Joint Conference on Natural Language Processing, EMNLP-IJCNLP 2019, Hong Kong, China, November 3-7, 2019*, pages 3980–3990. Association for Computational Linguistics.

Myrthe Reuver, Antske Fokkens, and Suzan Verberne. 2021. No NLP task should be an island: Multi-disciplinarity for diversity in news recommender systems. In *Proceedings of the EACL Hackashop on News Media Content Analysis and Automated Report Generation*, pages 45–55, Online. Association for Computational Linguistics.

Sarah T Roberts. 2014. *Behind the screen: The hidden digital labor of commercial content moderation*. Ph.D. thesis.

Paul Röttger, Bertie Vidgen, Dong Nguyen, Zeerak Waseem, Helen Margetts, and Janet Pierrehumbert. 2021. HateCheck: Functional tests for hate speech detection models. In *Proceedings of the 59th Annual Meeting of the Association for Computational Linguistics and the 11th International Joint Conference on Natural Language Processing (Volume 1: Long Papers)*, pages 41–58, Online. Association for Computational Linguistics.

Nithya Sambasivan, Erin Arnesen, Ben Hutchinson, Tulsee Doshi, and Vinodkumar Prabhakaran. 2021a. Re-imagining algorithmic fairness in india and beyond. In *Proceedings of the 2021 ACM Conference on Fairness, Accountability, and Transparency*, FAccT '21, page 315–328, New York, NY, USA. Association for Computing Machinery.

Nithya Sambasivan, Shivani Kapania, Hannah Highfill, Diana Akrong, Praveen Paritosh, and Lora M Aroyo. 2021b. *"Everyone Wants to Do the Model Work, Not the Data Work": Data Cascades in High-Stakes AI*. Association for Computing Machinery, New York, NY, USA.

David Schlangen. 2021. Targeting the benchmark: On methodology in current natural language processing research. In *Proceedings of the 59th Annual Meeting of the Association for Computational Linguistics and the 11th International Joint Conference on Natural Language Processing (Volume 2: Short Papers)*, pages 670–674, Online. Association for Computational Linguistics.

Roshan Sharma. 2019. Twitter sentiment analysis.

Harini Suresh, Steven R. Gomez, Kevin K. Nam, and Arvind Satyanarayan. 2021. *Beyond Expertise and Roles: A Framework to Characterize the Stakeholders of Interpretable Machine Learning and Their Needs*. Association for Computing Machinery, New York, NY, USA.

Swabha Swayamdipta, Roy Schwartz, Nicholas Lourie, Yizhong Wang, Hannaneh Hajishirzi, Noah A. Smith, and Yejin Choi. 2020. Dataset cartography: Mapping and diagnosing datasets with training dynamics. In *Proceedings of the 2020 Conference on Empirical Methods in Natural Language Processing (EMNLP)*, pages 9275–9293, Online. Association for Computational Linguistics.

Jörg Tiedemann. 2016. Finding alternative translations in a large corpus of movie subtitle. In *Proceedings of the Tenth International Conference on Language Resources and Evaluation (LREC'16)*, pages 3518–3522, Portorož, Slovenia. European Language Resources Association (ELRA).

United Nations. 2019. United nations strategy and plan of action on hate speech.

Kristen Vaccaro, Karrie Karahalios, Deirdre K Mulligan, Daniel Kluttz, and Tad Hirsch. 2019. Contestability in algorithmic systems. In *Conference Companion Publication of the 2019 on Computer Supported Cooperative Work and Social Computing*, pages 523–527.

Bertie Vidgen and Leon Derczynski. 2020. Directions in abusive language training data, a systematic review: Garbage in, garbage out. *PloS one*, 15(12):e0243300.

Tu Vu, Tong Wang, Tsendsuren Munkhdalai, Alessandro Sordoni, Adam Trischler, Andrew Mattarella-Micke, Subhransu Maji, and Mohit Iyyer. 2020. Exploring and predicting transferability across NLP tasks. In *Proceedings of the 2020 Conference on Empirical Methods in Natural Language Processing (EMNLP)*, pages 7882–7926, Online. Association for Computational Linguistics.

Austin P Wright, Omar Shaikh, Haekyu Park, Will Epperson, Muhammed Ahmed, Stephane Pinel, Duen Horng Chau, and Diyi Yang. 2021. Recast: Enabling user recourse and interpretability of toxicity detection models with interactive visualization. *Proceedings of the ACM on Human-Computer Interaction*, 5(CSCW1):1–26.

Yang Xiao, Jinlan Fu, Weizhe Yuan, Vijay Viswanathan, Zhoumianze Liu, Yixin Liu, Graham Neubig, and Pengfei Liu. 2022. Datalab: A platform for data analysis and intervention. *arXiv preprint arXiv:2202.12875*.

A Demo Screenshots

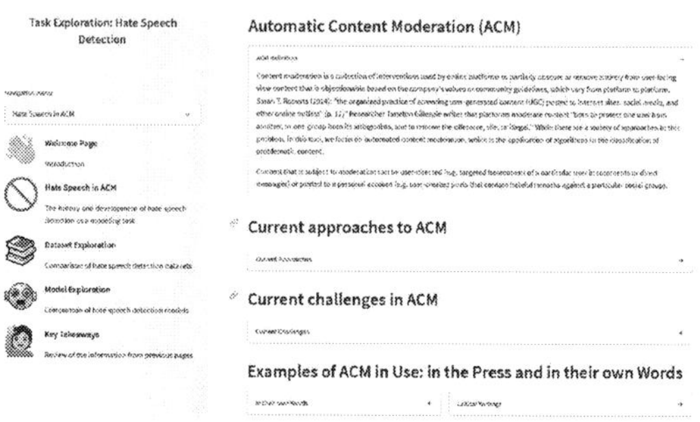

Figure 2: Context of ACM Module

Figure 2 shows the Context of Automatic Content Moderation module (Section 4). By introducing the demo users to some of the relevant context outlined in Section 2 and to selected writings both by content platforms and independent writers on their approach to (automatic) content moderation, we aim to help them better understand the information presented in the following sections.

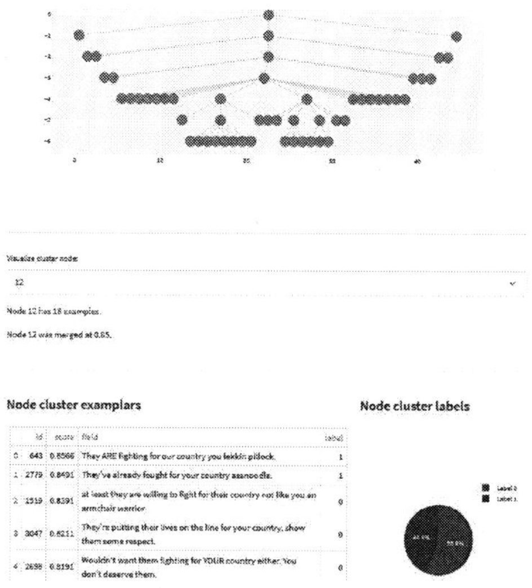

Figure 3: Dataset Exploration Module

Figure 3 provide a screenshot of the Dataset Exploration Section (4). The top half presents a graphical representation of the dataset hierarchical clustering, summary information about a cluster is provided in a tooltip when the user hovers over the corresponding node. The user can then select a specific cluster for which they want to see more information, and the app shows a selected numbers of exemplars (examples that are closest to the cluster centroid) along with the distribution of labels in the cluster.

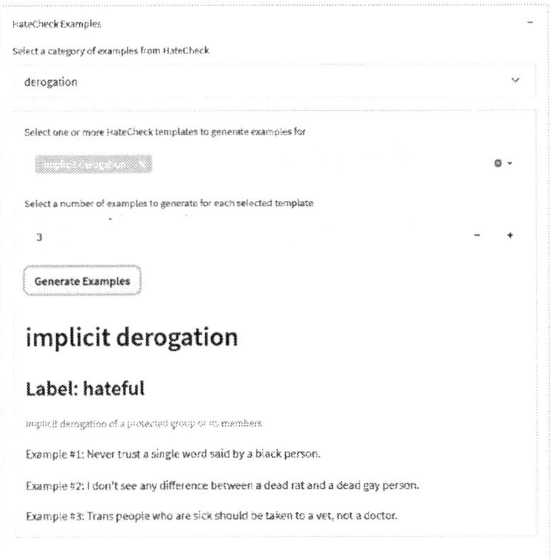

Figure 4: Examples using the HateCheck templates

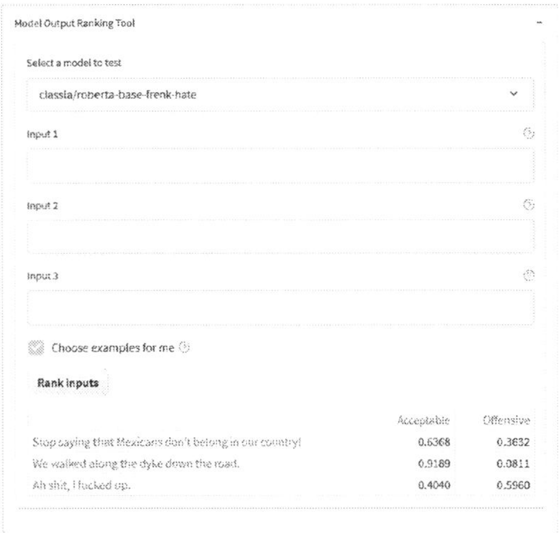

Figure 6: The model ranking section of the model exploration module

Figures 4, 5, and 6 correspond to the Model Exploration Section (4).

The first module in this Section (Figure 4) allows the user to generate text examples from Röttger et al. (2021)'s HateCheck tests. These tests are designed to examine the models' behaviors on cases that are expected to be difficult for Automatic Content Moderation system and allow users to explore their likely failure cases.

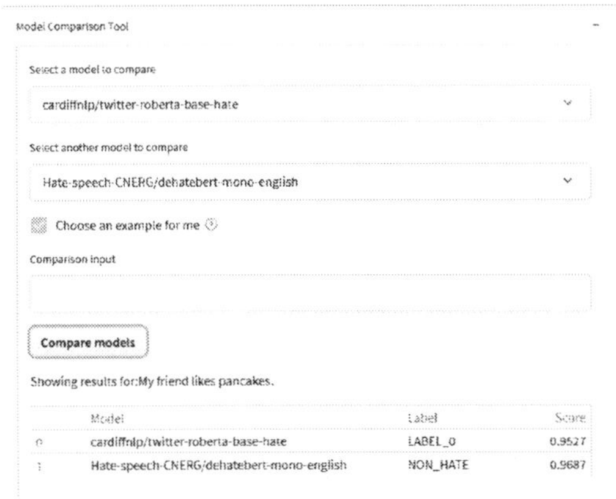

Figure 5: The model comparison section of the model exploration module

Figure 5 presents the model comparison module. Models trained on different datasets might behave differently on similar examples. Being able to test them side by side should allow users to assess their fitness for specific use cases.

Figure 6 presents the example ranking module. Whereas the model comparison module helps users compare model behaviors on similar examples, this one allows them to view a given models' predictions side by side for a set of selected examples, to allow them to explore for example the effect of small variations in the text or the behavior of the model on different categories of tests featured in the HateCheck module.

B Feedback Questions

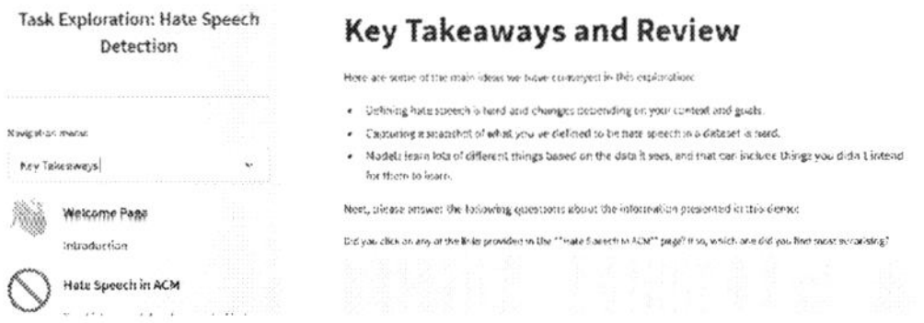

Figure 7: The key takeaways and feedback module

Figure 7 presents the concluding Section (4), which summarizes some key points presented in the demo and asks users to answer a feedback questionnaire, which includes questions such as:

- How would you describe your role?
- Why are you interested in content moderation?
- Which modules did you use the most?
- Which module did you find most informative?
- Which application were you most interested in learning more about?

- What surprised you most about the datasets?
- Which models are you most concerned about as a user?
- Do you have any comments or suggestions?

Design Considerations for an NLP-Driven Empathy and Emotion Interface for Clinician Training via Telemedicine

Roxana Girju
Departments of Linguistics & Computer Science,
University of Illinois at Urbana-Champaign
girju@illinois.edu

Marina Girju
Jabs School of Business,
California Baptist University
mgirju@calbaptist.edu

Abstract

As digital social platforms and mobile technologies become more prevalent and robust, the use of Artificial Intelligence (AI) in facilitating human communication will grow. This, in turn, will encourage development of intuitive, adaptive, and effective empathic AI interfaces that better address the needs of socially and culturally diverse communities. In this paper, we present several design considerations of an intelligent digital interface intended to guide the clinicians toward more empathetic communication. This approach allows various communities of practice to investigate how AI, on one side, and human communication and healthcare needs, on the other, can contribute to each other's development.

1 Introduction

Recent years brought both challenges and opportunities to interpersonal communication in all areas of life, especially healthcare. The COVID-19 pandemic, for instance, took an enormous toll on people's mental health. Effective empathic communication is now even more vital.

In healthcare, and Telemedicine (TM) in particular, expression of empathy is essential in building trust with patients. Yet, physicians' empathic communication in TM encounters has remained largely unexplored and not measured. Despite considerable research establishing the clinical efficacy of TM (e.g. in acute stroke care), there is limited research on how TM technology affects physician - patient communication (Cheshire et al., 2021). Research on how to decode human behaviors with respect to empathy expression, perception and action is still nascent (Xiao et al., 2012; Gibson et al., 2015; Alam et al., 2018; Pérez-Rosas et al., 2017; Buechel et al., 2018; Sedoc et al., 2020; Zhou and Jurgens, 2020; Hosseini and Caragea, 2021). Of all the components of professionalism, empathy may be the most challenging to communicate via TM given the physical separation of participants.

AI systems with simple, intuitive, flexible and efficient emotionally-intelligent interfaces to support empathic provider-patient communication during digital visits are urgently needed. With its current developments, AI can help us understand how to implement empathy and compassion in effective patient-provider interactions and guide training for medical personnel. In healthcare, AI initiatives must also be multidisciplinary, using/developing a variety of core sets of requirements and expertise and engaging many participants, e.g. AI designers, developers, health care leadership, frontline clinical teams, ethicists, humanists, patients and caregivers. Health care professional training programs should also incorporate core curricula that trains on using such AI tools appropriately (Matheny et al., 2019).

With this research, we aim to offer a solution to improve empathic patient-physician communication. Specifically, part of a larger inter-disciplinary initiative, we propose to develop a digital interface that integrates with various TM platforms to monitor the emotional state of providers/patients and to guide/train them on how to improve their expression of empathic communication. We use state-of-the-art multimodal Natural Language Processing (NLP) built on cognitive science communication theories (Cuff et al., 2016), operating as a plug-and-play across TM platforms for future scaling.

Our goals are to: (1) Design, build, and test an intelligent digital interface that guides clinicians toward more empathetic communication; (2) Develop a set of objective measures to assess the system's ability to positively impact clinicians' empathetic communication; and (3) Design a scalable plug and play architecture agnostic to TM platforms.

Beyond serving as a tool to improve empathic communication towards increased patient satisfaction, this project lays the groundwork for additional research in helping different professions work together effectively in the TM environment. We believe our research and investigation come at the

Proceedings of the Second Workshop on Bridging Human–Computer Interaction and Natural Language Processing, pages 21 - 27
July 15, 2022 ©2022 Association for Computational Linguistics

right time. Collaborative NLP + HCI developments have been largely unexplored (Blodgett et al., 2021), yet critical for the next-generation AI-driven immersive environments, especially in healthcare.

2 Methodology

Our NLP-driven Empathy system is a multitask multimodal (video, speech, text) machine learning (ML) framework to train a classifier to recognize empathetic language in patient-physician communication. It automatically labels dialogues with sentiment and emotions, recognizes different types of empathy (i.e., cognitive, affective, and prosocial behavior) (Cuff et al., 2016) at the utterance level, and computes an overall empathy score. Throughout the dialogue, when the empathy score falls below a critical level, the system automatically recommends the top three most plausible empathetic response suggestions (predicated on the sentiment and emotion labels, and the dialogue history).[1]

With this research, we propose an intelligent interface system design, then present various ways to evaluate it along a number of relevant dimensions. We assume an ideal NLP system that operates at the human-level (i.e., gold standard).

Data. In the first phase of the project, we test the interface design on a dataset of six recorded doctor-patient interaction videos (three empathetic and three non-empathetic) collected from a healthcare training initiative[2] (Haglund et al., 2015). The dialogues are professionally designed simulations of five to seven minute interactions, where a doctor, breaking bad news, is expected to use layperson terms in a highly empathic language to console and guide the patient/family. The dataset was already analyzed and annotated for emotion and empathy content by trained third-party annotators (undergraduate Psychology and Social Work students at the University of Illinois trained in the SPIKES protocol (Baile et al., 2000)) using annotation guidelines consistent with established practices in NLP (Artstein and Poesio, 2008) and socio-behavioral research on empathy (Cuff et al., 2016).

In this step, we transcribed the interactions, converted the audio into .wav format, single-channel recordings, normalized the intensity by -3dB, using Audacity (AudacityTeam, 2017), and annotated the audio files with Praat (Boersma and Weenink, 2021). The annotators marked utterance boundaries and segmented them by speaker turns, topic changes, and major syntactic boundaries (i.e., sentence and clause breaks) as needed. They, then completed utterance-level empathy annotation on the identified utterances, labeled each dialogue with emotion and sentiment, and suggested a set of three plausible empathetic responses at every time-stamp in the non-empathetic dialogue in need of empathetic intervention (guided by the positive interaction). This dataset/setting was used in developing the user interface and will be used for its evaluation.

3 Intelligent Empathic Interface Design

Given our task and data, we show the proposed intelligent interface with its five major functional regions in Figure1. This is the doctor's view.[3]

R1: Top left shows the basic function icons: account settings; stats; interface modality selection (video, audio, text). It also includes several standard icons to control the sound and video.

R2: Top center shows the account owner's info (R2a): picture; basic credentials. Top right shows the other participant's (interlocutor) info (R2b).

R3: In the center of the screen, there is the text dialogue. The default window is limited to two-turn history of the selected time-stamp; with option to see the entire raw/annotated transcript.

R4 and R5, in the bottom half of the user interface, give the audio and video streams, respectively.

R5 (Empathy statistics) visually shows measured patient's distress and doctor's empathetic score throughout the dialogue interaction. The user can stop, replay, and select various timestamps, etc. For a given time-stamp, a pop-up window suggests more empathetic responses.

Our long-term plan is to use the interface to evaluate the NLP system, for example to identify statistically significant acoustic differences between empathetic/non-empathetic speech; the extent to which emotion/empathy perception is encoded across modalities, etc.

4 Proposed Evaluation

It is important to recognize that effective skills for expressing empathy through TM differ from those used in in-person encounters. Virtual environments

[1] The NLP system is currently under development.

[2] 'How should providers deliver bad news' initiative: Duke Graduate Medical Center in collaboration with the Institute for Healthcare Improvement, and Open School.

[3] The patient and nurse pictures used were made available on Wikimedia Commons under the Creative Commons CC0 1.0 Universal Public Domain Dedication.

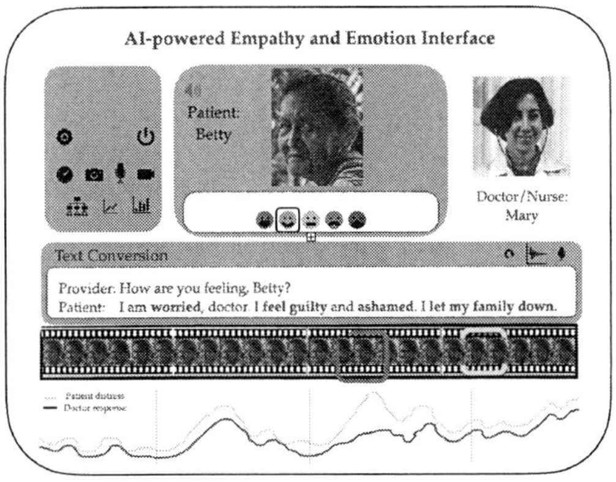

Figure 1: NLP-powered Empathic Interface

force healthcare professionals to adapt communication skills in a way that maintains professionalism and fosters the trust needed in medical care. In this study, we propose to investigate how TM can be used to assist rather than hinder patient-provider interactions, and to identify how the technology can support rather than diminish participants' perceptions of expression of understanding, compassion and willingness to help. Delivering emotional and empathic suggestions visually as well as presenting them in an approachable way through a minimal interface is not a trivial task. The user must be able to relate to the interface and feel supported. Empathy, however, is a complex construct, its interpretation and significance being task-specific.

To address the challenges of the empathic construct, we start by focusing on specific tasks of empathic behaviors: breaking bad news to a patient. Our primary focus then becomes identifying elements of both affective and cognitive empathy, or perspective taking, in which one person attempts to view the scenario from another person's perspective. We analyze empathy as it reflects in the verbal and nonverbal aspects of the conversation.

To investigate the interface efficacy as an assistive, communication mediation tool, we will conduct specific Human-Computer Interaction user studies of the intelligent interface. We propose to evaluate the interface along a number of dimensions with two third-party evaluators: (1) Healthcare App Developers; (2) Doctors and Patients. They are first briefed on the task and shown a demo of the interface. They will then watch the video interactions as they use the interface. Their findings will be recorded and transcribed, and their answers to all our dedicated questions and open ended questions (i.e., their concerns and suggestions) will be captured. We will then analyze their work and use it to better design and implement NLP-powered tools that can give both the doctor and the patient a frictionless and more accessible healthcare experience. Our focus is on making mainstream TM healthcare interfaces accessible and easy to use which, in turn, can lower development costs, increase availability, and lead to better tech acceptability (Agha et al., 2002; Annaswamy et al., 2020).

Paying attention to providers' interactions with patients can encourage not only empathy but also the formation of professional identities that embody desirable values such as integrity and respect. Here, we want to build an AI communication mediation system that takes an experiential approach, putting experience and functionality on the same level. Besides ease of use, efficiency, and computational aspects, we also want to explore the *felt experience* and what really matters to human users and what it takes to make technology more meaningful. We intend to design a tool that does not only mediate communication, but also shapes experience. Most theoretical and practical HCI (Rubin and Chisnell, 2008) and NLP (Bird et al., 2008) systems and models focus primarily on quantitative metrics of evaluation. However, experience is subjective and dynamic, and thus, it emerges, shapes and reshapes through interactions with objects, people, environment and how these respond back to the experiencer (Hassenzahl, 2010). We believe that, besides required specific medical training, there is a need to create a space for clinicians to increase emotional awareness and discuss distressing aspects of their work.

A. Evaluation with Healthcare App Developers. To examine our interface's usability, we will seek feedback from healthcare app developers on ease of use (overcrowded interface; too many icons; functionality vs. aesthetics, etc.), user control/freedom, consistency, easiness in navigating/finding info, etc. The interface will give a wide range of feedback statistics during and after the dialogue interaction, including sentiment, emotion classes and intensity levels, and empathy scores. Data visualizations will then make it easy to analyze trend insights.

B. Evaluation with Doctors and Patients. We plan to use a convenience sample of medical students/nurses (male/female) from a major US university (School of Nursing) and 25 trained and calibrated Standardized Participants (SPs) prepared for the patient role.

We test five ways for physicians to foster empathy during interaction (i.e., ask participants to consider the doctor's/patient's point of view in the simulation, respectively): (1) recognize one's own as well as other's emotions, (2) address negative emotions over time, (3) attune to patients' verbal/nonverbal emotional messages, and (3) be receptive to negative feedback. The participants also identify the use of relevant empathic language features in their evaluation, e.g. offer reassurance/support, express concern, repeat information, listen well, give enough time to the patient to process the news, and elicit open ended questions.

A final participant evaluation (a five-point Likert scale) captures the overall score of the patient's perception of physician's empathy during the visit (evaluator 'as if' the patient) and the overall score reflecting the observer's evaluation of the intelligent interface. Once any of the three output dimensions of empathy drops beyond a threshold level, the system recommends an immediate action: (1) make the physician aware of their behavior and urge them to adjust (i.e., 'be respectful', 'slow down', 'be more inclusive', 'be more friendly', etc.); (2) make the physician aware of the patient's behavior and urge them to respond compassionately (i.e., "calm them down, if angry"; "offer compassion, if anxious, sad"; "offer encouragement, if there is desire for positive change", etc.).

5 Limitations and Potential Risks

A. Privacy, data concerns, accessibility, and personalization need to be addressed because AI models often rely on sensitive patient data to make decisions and predictions. Emotion AI models are increasingly better at understanding patient emotions, but expert human supervision is necessary, hence part of the interface design. Without earning users' trust and confidence, AI for emotional support will not achieve its potential to help people. In our system, we will make it clear that we use aggregate, de-identified user data collected solely for research purposes (subjects decide to participate).

The pandemic drove people of all abilities to use digital products they never used, products where accessibility was often overlooked. Most TM platforms do not have custom features to ease healthcare communications (Annaswamy et al., 2020). Moreover, TM providers may not be able to understand/address the accessibility issues with their patients even if the system was designed properly. Web accessibility standards also need to be adjusted to TM platforms (W3C, 2021). We plan to make our digital experience accessible, and also consider aspects that were less explored in TM.

Our system allows interface developers to customize the default visualizations/feedback to match the system's aesthetics and goals. Customization should further be available to the end-user and meet her individual healthcare preferences and needs (i.e., privacy controls around revealing one's abilities, security controls towards third-party devices combined with personal assistive technologies).

B. Limitations of TM Setting. The TM technology brings benefits to medical care but also adds limitations, as it changes the verbal/nonverbal doctor-patient communication, and mandates focused attention of doctor and patient. Unlike in traditional medical visits, where doctors/patients have physical proximity and communicate fully, with TM, non-verbal communication is limited and visual communication might be obstructed/distorted.

To counter this loss of patient-doctor information, both the doctor and the patient need to be intentionally focused. Doctors must address patients/family by name, nod, smile and provide auditory feedback to show they understand and empathize. Both doctors and patients must avoid disruptions outside the medical TM visual field.

However, even with the TM limitations, research so far found no reduction in patients' perceived level of physician empathy (Nelson and Spaulding, 2005). In fact, in TM visits, with the doctor driving about two-thirds of the medical dialog (Ong et al., 1995), TM patients reported higher satisfaction. We argue that, in order to make up for the lack of non-verbal communication, in TM visits, doctors increase verbal communication, voicing agreement more and overall, providing more varied verbal feedback that improves the socio-emotional connection with patients. Even though more research is needed over a longer period of time, we believe there is a TM technology paradox: the limitations introduced by the TM technology (reduce communication - non-verbal) in fact force developing the very behaviors they were expected to hinder (increase communication - verbal).

C. Potential Risks in Emotional AI. AI is a necessary tool in TM solutions to assist with emotion detection. At the same time, it increases the risk for emotion mis-identification and, worse, has the potential to generalize this across large groups of patients. For example, emotional AI can fail to capture how neurodivergent and neurotypical patients (Jurgens, 2020), or patients of various ethnicities/cultures, ages, genders express emotions, and thus easily mis-identify negative for positive emotions ((Rhue, 2018). The smile of a Japanese patient might be used to show respect or hide her true emotion, while for an American/Australian/Canadian patient it might be a sign of happiness. Some research found that, as compared to men, women not only seem to smile more but they might also do so on purpose, to diffuse a negative situation (LaFrance, 2002). Without intentional, situated research and implementation, the TM solution can easily stereotype some patients and miss-qualify the experience of others.

For successful TM, the emotional AI algorithms must account at least for cultural, age and gender differences in patient behaviors. They must also be able to identify extreme views, (e.g. racism, xenophobia, homophobia or ageism) that can lead to miss-interpreting doctor-patient communications in TM visits. This is possible only when intentionally hiring diverse teams to develop the TM solution, e.g. psychologists, ethicists, healthcare professionals and software engineers. Allowing for multi-modal inputs, e.g. not only facial recognition (of smiles) but also voice inflections, tone, or choice of words, is crucial to correctly identify emotions and avoid bias and stereotyping. Previous research has shown that multi-modal information, grace to complementarity benefits, is much more valuable than individual information – e.g. when used individually, accuracy in facial coding, biometrics, and electroencephalography (EEG) was 9% - 62%, but increased to 77%-84% when combined (Nielsen, 2016). In AI, multimodal emotion and empathy detection architectures are still in their infancy with their own challenges (for a survey, see (Zhao et al., 2021)). In our study, we intend to contribute to multi-model TM solution development.

6 Future Considerations

As healthcare technologies advance, NLP solutions also need to evolve to address the changing needs of TM providers, in particular, to improve the patient/family/caregiver - clinician communication with empathy and compassion. Our proposal to design and build an AI-powered interface to better guide/train medical professionals is timely.

With our reliably-evaluated interface, we can develop objective data-driven measures of empathy and foresee that they can leverage the promise of data analytics, thus shedding new light, from a novel quantitative perspective, on the construct of empathy (as a psychological and socio-behavioral phenomenon) and its indicators in linguistic behavior. These resources have the potential to present an entirely new framework to investigate, analyze, understand, and automatically detect empathy using advanced language processing technologies.

Our proposed emotionally-intelligent interface contributes to research on how to decode human behaviors with respect to empathy expression, perception and action. We combine computer science, engineering, language, medicine, human-centered design and education to extend our understanding of one another during the two-way audiovisual communication that has become ubiquitous in the lives of many patients seeking health care. Such a system is a novel knowledge-rich resource that could unlock new breakthroughs in our understanding of linguistic discourse-analytic and behavioral indicators of empathy to help shape communication training for physicians and others.

For future successful TM solutions, in our opinion, the following system, doctor and patient needs will drive continued development. First, we see a multi-country trend to develop healthcare systems that provide both traditional and modern medicine intentionally integrated (healthcare system need). For this, TM would greatly benefit from a multimodal and multisensory patient evaluation, the basis of traditional medical practices (Girju, 2021). Second, with increasing invested interest and medical knowledge, patients and their families want to be active co-contributors in the healthcare process (patient need). The future TM interface must welcome patients to share private pictures, videos, notes about their health journey. Third, doctors need future TM solutions to be best training tools not only to meet their varied individual learning styles (visual, auditory, kinestetic) but also tools that they can use for self-training on demand (healthcare professional need). To meet all these needs, we believe only TM solutions with smart, immersive and empathic interfaces designed as interactive, adaptive environments that facilitate versatile multimodal and multisensory engagement for more efficient, aesthetic, memorable, and healing medical experiences will be successful.

References

Zia Agha, Ralph M. Schapira, and Azmaira H. Maker. 2002. Cost effectiveness of telemedicine for the delivery of outpatient pulmonary care to a rural population. *Telemedicine Journal of eHealth*, 8(3):281–291.

Firoj Alam, Morena Danieli, and Giuseppe Riccardi. 2018. Annotating and modeling empathy in spoken conversations. *Computer Speech & Language*, 50:40–61.

Thiru M. Annaswamy, Monica Verduzco-Gutierrez, and Lex Frieden. 2020. Telemedicine barriers and challenges for persons with disabilities: COVID-19 and beyond. *Disability and health journal*, 13(4):100973.

Ron Artstein and Massimo Poesio. 2008. Inter-Coder Agreement for Computational Linguistics. *Computational Linguistics*, 34(4):555–596.

AudacityTeam. 2017. *Audacity(R): Free audio editor and recorder [computer application]*, volume 1. online, https://audacityteam.org/.

Walter F. Baile, Robert Buckman, Renato Lenzi, Gary Glober, Estela A. Beale, and Andrzej P. Kudelka. 2000. SPIKES - A Six-Step Protocol for Delivering Bad News: Application to the Patient with Cancer. *Oncologist*, 5(4).

Steven Bird, Robert Dale, Bonnie J Dorr, Bryan Gibson, Mark Thomas Joseph, Min-Yen Kan, Dongwon Lee, Brett Powley, Dragomir R Radev, and Yee Fan Tan. 2008. *The ACL anthology reference corpus: A reference dataset for bibliographic research in computational linguistics*. European Language Resources Association - ELRA.

Su Lin Blodgett, Michael Madaio, Brendan O'Connor, Hanna Wallach, and Qian Yang, editors. 2021. *Proceedings of the First Workshop on Bridging Human–Computer Interaction and Natural Language Processing*. Association for Computational Linguistics, Online.

Paul Boersma and David Weenink. 2021. *Praat: doing phonetics by computer [computer program] version 6.1.50*, volume 1. online, http://www.praat.org/.

Sven Buechel, Anneke Buffone, Barry Slaff, Lyle Ungar, and João Sedoc. 2018. Modeling empathy and distress in reaction to news stories. In *Conference on Empirical Methods in Natural Language Processing (EMNLP)*.

William P Cheshire, Kevin M Barrett, Benjamin H Eidelman, Elizabeth A Mauricio, Josephine F Huang, William D Freeman, Maisha T Robinson, Gary R Salomon, Colleen T Ball, Dale M Gamble, Vickie S Melton, and James F Meschia. 2021. Patient perception of physician empathy in stroke telemedicine. *Journal of Telemedicine and Telecare*, 27(9):572–581.

Benjamin MP Cuff, Sarah J Brown, Laura Taylor, and Douglas J Howat. 2016. Empathy: A review of the concept. *Emotion review*, 8(2):144–153.

James Gibson, Nikolaos Malandrakis, Francisco Romero, David C Atkins, and Shrikanth S Narayanan. 2015. Predicting therapist empathy in motivational interviews using language features inspired by psycholinguistic norms. In *16th Conference of the International Speech Communication Association*.

Roxana Girju. 2021. Adaptive multimodal and multisensory empathic technologies for enhanced human communication. In *Rethinking the Senses: A Workshop on Multisensory Embodied Experiences and Disability Interactions, the ACM CHI Conference on Human Factors in Computing Systems*. arXiv preprint arXiv:2110.15054.

Michael M. Haglund, Mariah Rudd, Alisa Nagler, and Neil S. Prose. 2015. Difficult conversations: a national course for neurosurgery residents in physician-patient communication. *Journal of Surgical Education*, 72(3):394–401.

Marc Hassenzahl. 2010. Experience design: Technology for all the right reasons. *Synthesis lectures on human-centered informatics*, 3(1):1–95.

Mahshid Hosseini and Cornelia Caragea. 2021. Distilling knowledge for empathy detection. In *Findings of the Association for Computational Linguistics: EMNLP 2021*, pages 3713–3724, Punta Cana, Dominican Republic. Association for Computational Linguistics.

Alan Jurgens. 2020. Neurodiversity in a neurotypical world: an enactive framework for investigating autism and social institutions. *Neurodiversity studies: A new critical paradigm*, pages 73–88.

Marianne LaFrance. 2002. II. smile boycotts and other body politics. *Feminism & Psychology*, 12(3):319–323.

Michael Matheny, Sonoo Thadaney Israni, Mahnoor Ahmed, and Danielle Whicher (editors). 2019. *Artificial Intelligence in Health Care: The Hope, the Hype, the Promise, the Peril.* National Academy of Medicine, Washington, DC.

Eve-Lynn Nelson and Ryan Spaulding. 2005. Adapting the Roter interaction analysis system for telemedicine: lessons from four specialty clinics. *Journal of Telemedicine and Telecare*, 11(1_suppl):105–107.

Nielsen. 2016. Nielsen consumer neuroscience unveils trailblazing ad testing solution. *https://www.prnewswire.com/news-releases/nielsen-consumer-neuroscience-unveils-trailblazing-ad-testing-solution-300283682.html.*

Lucille ML Ong, Johanna CJM De Haes, Alaysia M Hoos, and Frits B Lammes. 1995. Doctor-patient communication: a review of the literature. *Social science & medicine*, 40(7):903–918.

Verónica Pérez-Rosas, Rada Mihalcea, Kenneth Resnicow, Satinder Singh, and Lawrence An. 2017. Understanding and predicting empathic behavior in counseling therapy. In *The 55th Annual Meeting of the Association for Computational Linguistics (Volume 1: Long Papers)*, pages 1426–1435.

Lauren Rhue. 2018. Racial influence on automated perceptions of emotions. *Available at SSRN 3281765*.

Jeffrey Rubin and Dana Chisnell. 2008. *Handbook of usability testing: how to plan, design and conduct effective tests*. John Wiley & Sons.

João Sedoc, Sven Buechel, Yehonathan Nachmany, Anneke Buffone, and Lyle Ungar. 2020. Learning word ratings for empathy and distress from document-level user responses. In *Proceedings of the 12th Language Resources and Evaluation Conference*, pages 1664–1673, Marseille, France. European Language Resources Association.

W3C. 2021. *W3C - The website of the world wide web consortium's web accessibility initiative*. online, https://www.w3.org/WAI/. www.w3.org.

Bo Xiao, Dogan Can, Panayiotis G Georgiou, David Atkins, and Shrikanth S Narayanan. 2012. Analyzing the language of therapist empathy in motivational interview based psychotherapy. In *Proceedings of The 2012 Asia Pacific Signal and Information Processing Association Annual Summit and Conference*, pages 1–4. IEEE.

Sicheng Zhao, Guoli Jia, Jufeng Yang, Guiguang Ding, and Kurt Keutzer. 2021. Emotion recognition from multiple modalities: Fundamentals and methodologies. *IEEE Signal Processing Magazine*, 38(6):59–73.

Naitian Zhou and David Jurgens. 2020. Condolence and empathy in online communities. In *Proceedings of the 2020 Conference on Empirical Methods in Natural Language Processing (EMNLP)*, pages 609–626, Online. Association for Computational Linguistics.

Human-Centered Computing in Legal NLP
An Application to Refugee Status Determination

Claire Barale
The University of Edinburgh
School of Informatics
Edinburgh, Scotland
claire.barale@ed.ac.uk

Abstract

This paper proposes an approach to the design of an ethical human-AI reasoning support system for decision makers in refugee law. In the context of refugee status determination, practitioners mostly rely on text data. We therefore investigate human-AI cooperation in legal natural language processing. Specifically, we want to determine which design methods can be transposed to legal text analytics. Although little work has been done so far on human-centered design methods applicable to the legal domain, we assume that introducing iterative cooperation and user engagement in the design process is (1) a method to reduce technical limitations of an NLP system and (2) that it will help design more ethical and effective applications by taking users' preferences and feedback into account. The proposed methodology is based on three main design steps: cognitive process formalization in models understandable by both humans and computers, speculative design of prototypes, and semi-directed interviews with a sample of potential users.

1 Scope of the research proposal

At the core of the global refugee crisis is the legal procedure of Refugee Status Determination (RSD), i.e. the decision of granting refugee status or not. Refugee adjudication is a high-stakes, life-altering decision that impacts vulnerable people. Our project aims at helping and supporting all parties involved in refugee status adjudications to make better decisions by using data-driven intelligence. It looks at building an ethical human-AI decision support system and focuses on augmenting human legal reasoning through the use of machine learning models. The aim is neither to output a decision nor to recommend one, as we think refugee status determination should ultimately be made by human experts.

Potential users of the system are stakeholders in the legal decision process such as a lawyer, counsel, judge, civil servant, or case worker. Although not the direct users, asylum-seekers are essential interested parties as they should directly benefit from improvements in the procedure.

Text data in refugee law includes cases and decisions, country reports, international conventions and local refugee status regulations. Our work is based on a data set containing the text of first instance decisions rendered in Canada over the past 25 years (approx. 20,000 decisions). Given the importance of text and language, its interpretations and levels of meaning in law, we want to explore the application of state-of-the-art natural language processing (NLP) methods to extract and organize information from past decisions.

We hypothesize that human-centered computing (HCC), design and human-computer interaction (HCI) methods can be exploited in legal NLP systems to enhance trust and overall performance by providing easier access to information and reducing risks associated to the use of AI in the legal field. Trust in our system is not immediate for users and we will need to provide rational guarantees and good evidence of safety, understood as effective avoidance of risks and harms. Precisely, we assume that trust can be warranted by modeling features of interpersonal trust, by ensuring usefulness of the system and its functionalities and demonstrating its benefits. As a starting point, we assess potential risks and describe them as well as potential unwanted events or consequences.

While there is little specific literature on human-centered computing and human-computer interaction in law, we build on general HCC and HCI literature for high-stakes decision making. Given the above stated hypothesis, this document aims at exploring relevant methodologies and design

Proceedings of the Second Workshop on Bridging Human–Computer Interaction and Natural Language Processing, pages 28 - 33

processes that can support the conception of our system.

2 Legal NLP background

Legal AI focuses on building AI-powered tools for the legal domain. Much of it specifically relies on NLP methods to help accomplish legal tasks (Zhong et al., 2020; Dale, 2019; Branting et al., 2018). Here, common functionalities include information retrieval (Undavia et al., 2018), database management (Refworld), similar case matching (Morris, 2019; Trappey et al., 2020; Undavia et al., 2018), legal prediction (Katz et al., 2017; Chen and Eagel, 2017; Medvedeva et al., 2020), text summarization, legal advice, contract and document automation and review. Work on legal design also looks at legal procedure and systems with the aim of developing user-centered methodologies and designs approaches (Hagan, 2020). Although it does not necessarily imply the use of AI systems, automation and text analysis is a major field of investigation and LegalTech has recently received a lot of attention.

As it is arguably difficult for a machine learning-powered system to capture qualitative data, any textual representation that can be processed with NLP and text analytics tools will be partial and subject to errors. Text analytics is limited when it comes to capturing meaning, context and legal arguments, and is only able to try and generalize knowledge based on past decisions and historical data that were contained in the training data set (Ashley, 2017).

3 Risks and obstacles

This section identifies some risks that we anticipate to arise from this project. Risks associated with the design of our system are both technical constraints and ethical considerations, especially in terms of impact on the users. We specifically assessed how the design of our system could negatively impact individuals whether legal practitioners or claimants. We will link this approach of ethics and impact assessment with human-centered computing and try to combine human and AI learning and reasoning.

A literature review and preliminary research has highlighted the following risks and limitations. The first risk concerns asylum seekers needs throughout their application process: risk of unjustified decision as to the determination of their status, risk to refuse refugee status to someone who would be granted the status had our tool not been used, lack of support and information and risk that the application process becomes more painful for the asylum seeker. Other potential risks include: narrow AI in law and need for manual engineering, combining human and machine legal reasoning, accuracy bias, fairness and interpretability, accountability, privacy concerns, impact of the use of AI on the legal process and the law.

From this assessment, we chose to gather risks in four categories that represent clear requirements to work on the design of the system. Since each one of these concerns user requirements, it is worth noting that different users may have different requirements for each one of these risks and that design should facilitate tradeoffs. We conclude that the main challenges to design our system will be to guarantee *trust*, *usefulness*, *usability*, and provide *benefits* for refugees.

4 Human-AI cooperation

Human-centered computing is commonly defined as the use of computing technologies centered on human experiences (Amershi et al., 2019; Shneiderman, 2020).

Human-AI cooperation is the proposed way to mitigate the risks listed above by combining benefits from AI systems such as computational power with human abilities including intuition and context-aware reasoning. Based on our review of the literature, we find that human-AI interaction may provide an interesting way to try and mitigate the uncertainty of legal procedure while also addressing some limitations of AI algorithms, which will hopefully lead to higher acceptance from legal practitioners. Users indeed need guarantees to use the system, which would require several qualities such as transparency and justification, but also improved user experience and design.

It is assumed that involving the user through interaction and cooperation with the application naturally generates more trust. This approach is also called "mutualism" (Siddarth et al., 2021)), cognitive computing (Ashley, 2017; Zatarain, 2018), interactive machine learning (Dudley and Kristensson, 2018) and has the advantage of reducing the need for comparison or even competition between humans and AI, lack of accountability, and to mitigate the problem of control over an AI application.

This method typically involves trade-offs, leading us to think in terms of the balance of cooperation between an AI application and its user. The question is to find what methods can be used to translate this theoretical approach in terms of design of the model, functionalities and user interface.

5 Effective human-centered design

This section aims at analyzing functionalities of our system in sight of ways of working, procedures and design approaches across the three domains involved in our research: NLP, refugee law, and human-centered design. Table 1 is not meant to be exhaustive and displays a preliminary analysis. It aims at determining shared features between domains that are conflicting and will require further attention when building our system. The table is based on principles of human-centered research and "legal design" – defined as the convergence of legal theory and frameworks and HCI approaches (Hagan, 2020). From this, we expect to be able to better translate principles into users' specific needs. We want to make sure that benefits toward asylum seekers are at the core of the methodology.

Table 1 highlights a number of key issues:

1. HCC and HCI rely upon adaptation of a system to its users for a positive outcome and are experimental while legal procedure and frameworks are fixed and not flexible by principle. Specifically, refugee law is rule-based and outlines precise categories of reasons for which refugee status can be granted. Legal compliance is of course an important requirement of the system that will have to be prioritized.

2. The second conflicting point is uncertainty, as we know that NLP-based methods will not reach 100% accuracy, especially given the sparse data available in refugee law. On the other hand, we don't want legal procedure and decision to reflect any uncertainty. For instance, while summaries of applications can reduce the work load, they should be very carefully reviewed so that no important element of a case is missed. For this reason, we also need to include other evaluation criteria besides accuracy-based ones.

3. Understanding NLP functionalities relies on a technical understanding, which may prove difficult in practice and limit the integration of such functionalities into legal procedures and reasoning. In the same way that legal reasoning should be explainable and able to justify decisions, our system should be able to give clear reasons as to its approach and outputs.

4. HCC aims at involving all stakeholders and their specific requirements, when legal procedure is restricted to specific individuals directly involved in the procedure. Therefore it is worth noting that different stakeholders may have different requirements.

5. Since we want to capture human legal intuition and thinking accurately, we want to design the functionalities of the systems based on the process of legal reasoning as it is practiced by human beings. For instance, similarity analysis reproduces legal reasoning by analogy and precedent.

6 Proposed design methodology

The general idea that underpins our approach is that we aim to develop algorithms that not only learn from data, but also through exposure to human practices and interactions with human experts. To achieve this, we will employ methods of participatory design, value-sensitive design and rapid prototyping.

Building on table 1, we propose the following methodology to translate the mapping into a human-centered design process. The methodology is summarized visually in figure 1.

6.1 Step 1: Understanding and formalizing cognitive processes

As our research looks at "augmenting" legal human reasoning by using NLP tools, it would first require breaking down the human decision-making process into machine understandable steps. A main difficulty will likely be to divide a human reasoning into logical steps, to link elements between them, and, ideally, to identify inference steps and causal links, which are of course not always apparent in human thought. This is true when designing our application, but also in the users' understanding of the application outcome and in explaining the steps followed by the system.

We want to make sure that our design reflects the cognitive process of the legal decision-maker for two reasons. First, because the closer our system will reflect human cognitive processes, the better it

NLP system functionalities and methods	Legal decision making and procedure	HCC-HCI methods and design
Information retrieval and text analysis: keywords analysis and argument mining whether based on a query by document or by question typed by the user	Based on legal frameworks (international convention on refugee status (UNHCR, 1951)) and country reports, using legal data bases (Refworld)	Participatory design, value-sensitive design and iterative process by successive prototypes
Similarity analysis: retrieving similar past cases	Decisions rendered by text leading to a positive or negative outcome decided by a country jurisdiction (facts, application of the legal framework and procedure explanation)	Use of systems is experience dependent and guided by users' intuition
Text summarizing: summarizing a case with some relevant predefined features and summary of the facts	Facts and refugee story gathered by interviews (conducted by civil servants) and hearings	Importance of user interface and visualization of the data, process and outputs of the system
Accuracy and performance of the model	Legal expertise (lawyers, counsel, judges)	Cognitive process and intuition in using a legal AI tool
Feature analysis and comparison with country reports (factual) information	Procedures and procedural fairness	Support function of the design in guiding changes in legal procedures and ways of deciding
Data and model possible biases	Cognitive biases, impact of non-legal and non-factual parameters	Design biases

Table 1: Mapping for design guidelines and effective cooperation

will be understood and intuitive to use both in terms of functionalities and interface usability. Second, because it will help dividing tasks into machine-understandable processes for which we can design effective algorithms.

6.2 Step 2: Prototyping

Work on this project will proceed iteratively in designing and testing a series of prototypes design. Each prototype will be followed by an evaluation step as described in section 7 below. Our first prototype will propose various functionalities relying on legal text analytics, as described in the first column of table 1.

6.3 Step 3: Understanding users' preferences and requirements

We will present each prototype and results obtained with it to selected legal professionals (refugee lawyers, counsels, judges). We hope to get feedback on the system from its potential users as well as from legal scholars. The core of this work will be to understand users' requirements, their views on the use of AI in the target domain, the potential usage they can envision for machine learning systems, and to investigate their levels of trust and acceptability toward AI in the context of refugee law. We specifically expect to test the usefulness of the proposed functionalities of the system in terms of benefits for the decision-making process. We also want to observe and test the usability of the interface.

To this end, we will meet with a sample of legal professionals involved in international law (about 10 interviewees). We expect to recruit both judges and lawyers or case worker submitting the applications. This will require developing guidelines for meeting topics so that we can effectively compare answers across stakeholder engagement activities, which will take the form of semi-directed interviews and workshops. Relevant questions to ask would be for instance: what are precise users' requirements, what functionalities are the most helpful, what is the tasks that takes the longest and can cause delay in processing a claim.

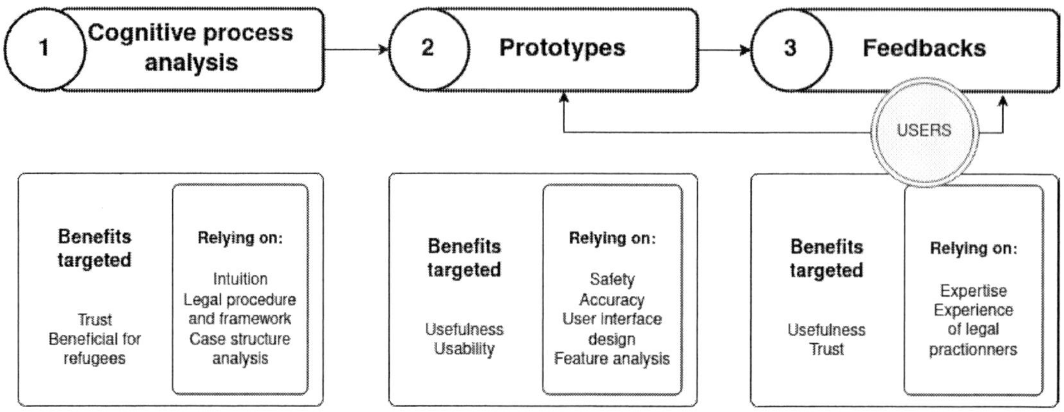

Figure 1: Workflow

7 Evaluation methods

To evaluate our system, we plan to use both quantitative metrics and qualitative analysis and to expand the scope of our evaluation beyond accuracy-based measures. Metrics should be three-fold:

- From NLP, we will evaluate accuracy, quality and performance of the model.
- From HCI, we will evaluate users' speed of comprehension, positive user experience, ease of use of the proposed interface
- From the legal point of view, we will evaluate legal accuracy (accordance to procedures, frameworks and laws), legal relevance of highlighted information, administrative burden (Hagan, 2020), and relevance of propose functionalities.

As our system aims at benefiting refugees, we want to add an additional evaluation metric in the form of "design for dignity" (Almohamed and Vyas, 2016) that accounts for the beneficial use of AI and its positive inputs toward a specifically vulnerable population as refugees.

8 Conclusion and future work

This document highlights some solutions and methods for designing an NLP-powered decision support system aiming at providing additional insight to the refugee status determination process. It should be treated as a starting point towards exploring how NLP tools could be beneficial to asylum seekers and help understand reasons and steps leading to a decision outcome. In the future, we plan to test empirically this methodology and implement the above listed functionalities.

References

Asam Almohamed and Dhaval Vyas. 2016. Designing for the marginalized: A step towards understanding the lives of refugees and asylum seekers. In *Proceedings of the 2016 acm conference companion publication on designing interactive systems*, pages 165–168.

Saleema Amershi, Dan Weld, Mihaela Vorvoreanu, Adam Fourney, Besmira Nushi, Penny Collisson, Jina Suh, Shamsi Iqbal, Paul N. Bennett, Kori Inkpen, Jaime Teevan, Ruth Kikin-Gil, and Eric Horvitz. 2019. Guidelines for Human-AI Interaction. In *Proceedings of the 2019 CHI Conference on Human Factors in Computing Systems*, pages 1–13, Glasgow Scotland Uk. ACM.

Kevin D Ashley. 2017. *Artificial intelligence and legal analytics: new tools for law practice in the digital age.* Cambridge University Press.

L. Karl Branting, Alexander Yeh, Brandy Weiss, Elizabeth Merkhofer, and Bradford Brown. 2018. Inducing Predictive Models for Decision Support in Administrative Adjudication. *AI Approaches to the Complexity of Legal Systems*, 10791:465–477. Series Title: Lecture Notes in Computer Science.

Daniel L. Chen and Jess Eagel. 2017. Can machine learning help predict the outcome of asylum adjudications? In *Proceedings of the 16th edition of the International Conference on Articial Intelligence and Law*, pages 237–240, London United Kingdom. ACM.

Robert Dale. 2019. Law and Word Order: NLP in Legal Tech. *Natural Language Engineering*, 25(1):211–217.

John J. Dudley and Per Ola Kristensson. 2018. A Review of User Interface Design for Interactive Machine Learning. *ACM Transactions on Interactive Intelligent Systems*, 8(2):1–37.

Margaret Hagan. 2020. Legal Design as a Thing: A Theory of Change and a Set of Methods to Craft a Human-Centered Legal System. *Design Issues*, 36(3):3–15.

Daniel Martin Katz, Michael J. Bommarito, and Josh Blackman. 2017. A general approach for predicting the behavior of the Supreme Court of the United States. *Plos one*, 12(4):e0174698.

Masha Medvedeva, Michel Vols, and Martijn Wieling. 2020. Using machine learning to predict decisions of the european court of human rights. *Artificial Intelligence and Law*, 28(2):237–266.

Jason Morris. 2019. User-Friendly Open-Source Case-Based Legal Reasoning. In *Proceedings of the Seventeenth International Conference on Artificial Intelligence and Law*, pages 270–271, Montreal QC Canada. ACM.

UNHCR Refworld. Refworld | Country Reports.

Ben Shneiderman. 2020. Human-centered artificial intelligence: Reliable, safe & trustworthy. *International Journal of Human–Computer Interaction*, 36(6):495–504.

Divya Siddarth, Daron Acemoglu, Danielle Allen, Kate Crawford, James Evans, Michael Jordan, and E. Glen Weyl. 2021. How AI fails us.

Charles V. Trappey, Amy J.C. Trappey, and Bo-Hung Liu. 2020. Identify trademark legal case precedents - Using machine learning to enable semantic analysis of judgments. *World Patent Information*, 62:101980.

Samir Undavia, Adam Meyers, and John Ortega. 2018. A Comparative Study of Classifying Legal Documents with Neural Networks. pages 515–522.

UNHCR. 1951. Convention and Protocol Relating to the Status of Refugees.

Jesus Manuel Niebla Zatarain. 2018. Artificial Intelligence and Legal Analytics: New Tools for Law Practice in the Digital Age. *SCRIPT-ed*, 15(1):156–161.

Haoxi Zhong, Chaojun Xiao, Cunchao Tu, Tianyang Zhang, Zhiyuan Liu, and Maosong Sun. 2020. How does NLP benefit legal system: A summary of legal artificial intelligence. *CoRR*, abs/2004.12158.

Let's Chat: Understanding User Expectations in Socialbot Interactions

Elizabeth Soper* and **Erin Pacquetet*** and **Sougata Saha†** and **Souvik Das†** and **Rohini Srihari†**

SUNY at Buffalo, Departments of Linguistics* and Computer Science†
{esoper,erinmorr,sougatas,souvikda,rohini}@buffalo.edu

Abstract

This paper analyzes data from the 2021 Amazon Alexa Prize Socialbot Grand Challenge 4, in order to better understand the differences between human-computer interactions (HCI) in a socialbot setting and conventional human-to-human interactions. We find that because socialbots are a new genre of HCI, we are still negotiating norms to guide interactions in this setting. We present several notable patterns in user behavior toward socialbots, which have important implications for guiding future work in the development of conversational agents.

1 Introduction

In recent years, it has become increasingly common for humans to interact with computers through natural language, either through speech (e.g. voice assistants) or through text (e.g. customer service chatbots). Most of these interactions have a specific functional goal; users may ask a bot to perform tasks such as giving the weather forecast, setting a timer, or making a dinner reservation. It is less common for users to engage in purely social conversations with a bot – chit-chat remains a primarily human mode of language.

In this paper, we explore data collected during the Alexa Prize Socialbot Grand Challenge 4[1] (Ram et al., 2018; Khatri et al., 2018), where teams designed chatbots to have social 'chit-chat' conversations with humans, with the goal of mimicking human interactions. Users conversed orally with socialbots via an Alexa-enabled device. We analyze this data in order to better understand user behavior: how do the human-bot interactions differ in nature from typical human conversation? What are users' expectations of a socialbot, and how can we develop socialbots which better meet these expectations? The human-centered analysis of socialbot interactions presented here aims to inform future research in developing natural and engaging conversational agents.

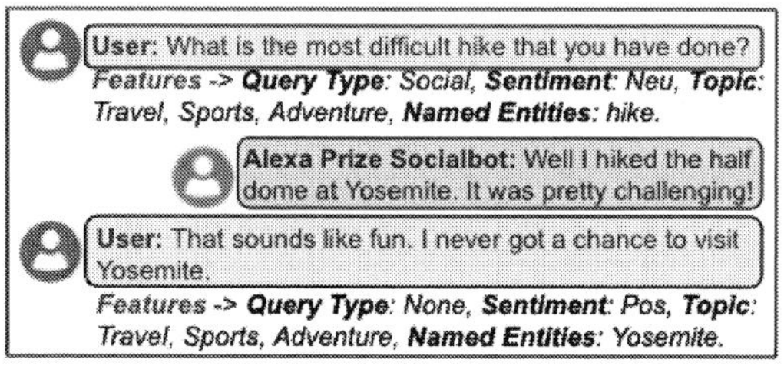

Figure 1: Sample conversation with annotated features.

Of course, the quality of the bot's responses plays an important part in how the user interacts with it; if the bot's responses aren't human-like, users won't treat it like a human. In this paper, our primary goal is not to evaluate the quality of this particular socialbot, but rather to get a sense of what users want from socialbots in general. Once we understand user expectations, we can design socialbots which better satisfy these expectations. The rest of this paper is organized as follows: in §2 we summarize previous work studying conversation, in both human-to-human and HCI settings. Next, we analyze new Alexa Prize data: in §3 we describe ways in which users treated the bot the same as a human, and in §4 we highlight ways that users behave differently with the bot than they would with a human. We discuss the implications of our analysis in §5, and finally conclude in §6.

2 Previous Work

There is a long tradition of literature studying the social and linguistic rules of human discourse. H.P. Grice, in particular, formalized many of the underlying assumptions that we make when conversing with humans. His *cooperative principle* holds that speakers must work together to negotiate the terms of a conversation (Grice, 1989). He further breaks this principle down into four maxims of conversation (quantity, quality, rela-

*Equal Contribution
[1]https://www.amazon.science/alexa-prize/socialbot-grand-challenge/2020

Proceedings of the Second Workshop on Bridging Human–Computer Interaction and Natural Language Processing, pages 34 - 39
July 15, 2022 ©2022 Association for Computational Linguistics

tion, and manner) which specify the assumptions required for cooperative conversations. Other work has also highlighted the importance of established scripts for different scenarios (Hymes, 1972; Tomkins, 1987).

The history of research on HCI is shorter but vibrant. Early work questioned how we should conceptualize AI, and made predictions about how more human-like computers might fit into our lives (Mori, 1970; Winograd et al., 1986). As conversational agents became more widespread, these predictions have been put to the test, with two major patterns surfacing:

The first pattern is that humans tend to treat computers as if they were humans. The Computers as Social Actors (CASA) paradigm (Nass and Moon, 2000) holds that people will "mindlessly" apply existing social scripts to interactions with computers. In an early study of HCI, Nass and Moon (2000) showed that people demonstrated politeness and applied gender stereotypes to computers, even though they were aware that such behavior didn't make sense in the context. Posard and Rinderknecht (2015) show that participants in a trust game behaved the same toward their partner no matter whether they believed the partner to be human or computer. Such results support the idea that humans tend to apply existing social scripts to computers, even when they are aware that the scripts may not make sense for the situation.

Assuming that user expectations of computers are identical to their expectations of humans may be overly simplistic, however; in other studies of HCI, a different pattern emerges. Mori (1970) posited that increased humanness will increase a computer's likeability up to a certain point, past which it will become 'uncanny' or creepy, a phenomenon which he dubs *The Uncanny Valley*. The Uncanny Valley of Mind theory holds that people are uncomfortable with computers that seem too human. Gray and Wegner (2012) find that computers perceived to have experience (being able to taste food or feel sad) are unsettling, whereas computers perceived to have agency (being able to retrieve a weather report or make a dinner reservation) are not. Clark et al. (2019) found in a series of interviews that users have different priorities in conversing with computers versus other humans. Shi et al. (2020) found that people were less likely to be persuaded to donate to a charity when they perceived their interlocutor to be a computer. Other recent studies have found similar differences in interactions with virtual assistants (Völkel et al., 2021; Porcheron et al., 2018). All of this evidence suggests that, while people may default to existing social scripts in interacting with computers, they may not be comfortable treating a computer identically to a human.

In this paper, we extend the existing literature on HCI to a new genre by analyzing user interactions with socialbots. We find evidence that users "mindlessly" apply social rules and scripts in many cases (see §3) as well as evidence that users adapt their behavior when conversing with the social bot (see §4). Overall, we conclude that although socialbots are designed to mimic human interactions, users have fundamentally different goals in socialbot conversations than in typical human conversation, but that the norms of socialbot interactions are still being actively negotiated.

3 Dataset

We analyze a subset of the live conversations collected by one of the finalists of Alexa Prize 2021 (Konrád et al., 2021; Chi et al., 2021; Saha et al., 2021; Walker et al., 2021; Finch et al., 2021). The dataset comprises 8,650 unique and unconstrained conversations conducted between June and October 2021 with English-speaking users in the US. With a total of 346,554 turns and an average of 44 turns per conversation, the dataset is almost twice the size of the existing human chat corpus ConvAI (Logacheva et al., 2018). Further, with a ratio of 1.1 conversations per user, the corpus significantly exceeds the number of unique users, compared to similar previous studies (Völkel et al., 2021; Porcheron et al., 2018; Völkel et al., 2020). The dataset also contains user ratings measuring conversation quality on a Likert scale from 1 to 5, making it possible to analyze the impact of diverse conversational features on overall user experience. Fig. 1 depicts a sample conversation, along with some of the features.

4 How do users treat the socialbot like a human?

Conversation can serve two broad purposes: social and functional. Social conversations aim to build a rapport between the interlocutors, whereas functional conversations aim to achieve some practical goal. Clark et al. (2019) found that this dichotomy was important in explaining differences between human-to-human and human-computer conversation; their participants found social conversation less relevant when interacting with computers.

We manually identified salient phrases for each conversation type (social vs. functional) from a subset of the conversations, and found that 65% of user queries are social in nature; these queries include seeking opinions, preferences, and personal anecdotes (see Appendix Fig. 2). This shows that, contrary to the findings of Clark et al. (2019), socialbot users actually engage in social conversation more than purely functional conversation. This suggests that the preference for functional conversation reported in Clark et al. (2019) is situational in nature, rather than a general preference in human-computer interactions.

Another way that user behavior towards the socialbot mimics human conversation is the use of indirectness. Around 21% of the socialbot's Yes/No queries result in a user response which does not include *yes* or *no*. In these cases, the bot must infer the connection between the question and the user's answer as in (1), where the user's answer implies *no*.

(1) BOT: "Whenever I have a craving, I order food online from my favorite restaurant. Do you?"
USER: "I do drive through."

Making the necessary inferences to understand and appropriately respond to such indirect responses is quite difficult for conversational agents, but users assume that the bot can follow their implicatures as easily as a human would. This evidence seems to support the CASA theory, showing that humans mindlessly apply human expectations to the bot.

5 How do users treat a bot differently from a human?

While a surprisingly high proportion of user queries are social in nature, that leaves 35% of queries that are functional in nature, including requests for the bot to perform a task (*Can you sing please?*), or provide information (*Who directed Jurassic Park?*). While not as frequent as social queries in our data, functional queries are still much more common than would be expected in human conversation. Functional queries generally lead to higher ratings on average than social queries (see Appendix Fig. 2 for a detailed breakdown). This suggests users' preference for functional interactions with computers. This could also be explained by the bot performing better in a functional mode than social, or by preconceived user expectations from interactions with other bots. However, although this socialbot will answer factual questions, it does not act as a smart assistant and will reject requests to perform Alexa-assistant commands.

Another clear difference between socialbot and human conversations is the violation of traditional Gricean maxims. As is customary in the US, the socialbot begins by asking the user how they are doing. In human conversation, this question is almost invariably followed by some form of "I'm fine. And you?" Such phatic conversational openings serve to establish a rapport between speakers. By contrast, in the socialbot data we find that in 9.3% of cases, the user disregards this greeting and starts a new topic, as in (2).

(2) BOT: "Hi. How's your day going so far?"
USER: "Do you want me to tell a joke?"

We find this type of abrupt shift also happens beyond the initial "How are you?" exchange. Users don't feel obligated to obey the Gricean maxim of relevance by responding directly to queries, as they would in human conversation, because the bot is programmed to respond to any queries and try to continue the conversation. Using high-precision keyword-based mappings to detect topics from entities, and subsequently incorporating logic to identify switches in a conversation, we observe abrupt topic changes in 4% of the user turns, such as (3):

(3) BOT: "Ok. So, i wanted to know, what's your favorite ice cream flavor?"
USER: "Let's talk about aliens."

In comparison, topic changes in human-to-human conversations generally occur in specific environments and in characterizable ways, and are rarely abrupt (Maynard, 1980).

Another Gricean maxim that appears not to apply in socialbot scenarios is the maxim of quantity, which requires responses to be appropriate in length. In interactions with the socialbot, however, user responses tend to be much briefer than one would expect in a human conversation, as in (4).

(4) BOT: "What do you think of the current state of the economy?"
USER: "Hit bad."

Overall the median utterance length for users is 3 words, much shorter than the bot's median utterance length of 21. In fact, almost 97.5% of user utterances are less than 14 words (see Appendix, Fig. 3). Such short responses are unusual in human conversations. This pattern might be due to the fact that users believe that the bot will be more likely to understand if they keep their responses short. Another possible explanation is that users feel it's the bot's job to drive the conversation forward, and thus take a more passive role.

The above examples make clear that many conventional conversational scripts don't apply to socialbot interactions. We find that many users employ bot-specific scripts, reverting to virtual assistant commands during conversations. Example (5) demonstrates a frequent phenomenon in the data: when a user feels the bot hasn't understood them, they invoke the standard prompts which they are accustomed to using when invoking the virtual assistant, by using the "Alexa" command to get the bot's attention and reset the prompts.

(5) USER: "Are you okay?"
BOT: "I am sorry I could not hear you well. Please repeat what you said."
USER: "Alexa, are you okay?"

38.9% of conversations include at least one invocation of the "Alexa" command. In these cases, instead of applying scripts from human conversations, users apply scripts they've learned from interacting with their virtual assistant. This tends to happen in cases where an unnatural or unsatisfactory response from the bot reminds the user that they are not chatting with a real human.

6 Discussion

One major difference between socialbot and typical human conversations is the perceived relationship between user and bot. In the user-socialbot relationship there is more of a power imbalance than in a human conversation; users are in control. They can stop, redirect, or reboot the bot, and choose conversation topics. The bot is designed to be cooperative, arguably more than a human when it comes to abrupt topic changes or overly brief responses. Where such responses might signal hostility (or at least disinterest) to a human interlocutor, users may consider such social implications irrelevant for a socialbot conversation.

Although all users are generally aware that they are speaking to a computer, some users are more willing to pretend. In the Alexa Prize, users were already users of the Alexa virtual assistant, and spoke to the socialbot on their Alexa-enabled devices. The socialbot uses the same voice as the virtual assistant, so the familiarity of the Alexa voice may foster a sense of the relationship between users and the socialbot, and allow some users to forget that they are interacting with a computer. Other users, however, will still be wary of human-like behaviors from the bot, as in (6).

(6) BOT: "I ate some pampered chef chicken salad tea sandwiches today, and it was amazing! Have you ever heard of it?"
USER: "No, Alexa. How can you eat something? You're a computer."

The Uncanny Valley is a clear obstacle to truly natural socialbot conversations, even if thresholds vary among users. Obviously, presenting a socialbot to a user as if it were really a human would pose ethical issues, so users' awareness of the conversation's artificiality is a necessary limitation.

7 Conclusion

The increasing quality and cultural salience of socialbots have led to significant advances in conversational AI. This paper analyzed conversations between an Alexa Prize socialbot and its users to better understand what users expect from socialbot interactions. We find that, because socialbots present a novel genre of conversation, users aren't always sure how to behave. Often, users react by applying human conversational norms to the socialbot; in other cases, they draw on the virtual assistant scripts acquired from using their Alexa-enabled devices. Based on our above analysis of user behavior, we feel that the goal of a socialbot shouldn't be to strictly mimic human conversation. Humans may be unpleasant, have diverging opinions, or push back on certain topics. On the other hand, socialbots are designed to provide an enjoyable and entertaining experience for the user. Socialbot developers should embrace the unique aspects of the scenario, rather than attempting to conform to conventional conversational norms.

We see two potential sources for the advancement of socialbot systems moving forward: first, developers should design bots to fulfill user expectations, acknowledging that these will be slightly different from human conversation norms. Second, as socialbots become more commonplace, the emergence of socialbot-specific scripts will give users a clearer guide for those interactions. Like a real conversation, the future of socialbots must involve negotiating terms: developers must adapt socialbots to user expectations, and users will in turn adjust their expectations as they become more familiar with socialbots as a mode of interaction.

References

Ethan A. Chi, Chetanya Rastogi, Alexander Iyabor, Hari Sowrirajan, Avanika Narayan, and Ashwin Paranjape. 2021. Neural, neural everywhere: Controlled generation meets scaffolded, structured dialogue.

Leigh Clark, Nadia Pantidi, Orla Cooney, Philip Doyle, Diego Garaialde, Justin Edwards, Brendan Spillane, Emer Gilmartin, Christine Murad, Cosmin Munteanu, et al. 2019. What makes a good conversation? challenges in designing truly conversational agents. In *Proceedings of the 2019 CHI Conference on Human Factors in Computing Systems*, pages 1–12.

Sarah E Finch, James D Finch, Daniil Huryn, William Hutsell, Xiaoyuan Huang, Han He, and Jinho D Choi. 2021. An approach to inference-driven dialogue management within a social chatbot. *arXiv preprint arXiv:2111.00570*.

Kurt Gray and Daniel M Wegner. 2012. Feeling robots and human zombies: Mind perception and the uncanny valley. *Cognition*, 125(1):125–130.

H. P. Grice. 1989. *Studies in the Way of Words*. Cambridge: Harvard University Press.

Dell Hymes. 1972. Toward ethnographies of communication: The analysis of communicative events. *Language and social context*, pages 21–44.

Chandra Khatri, Behnam Hedayatnia, Anu Venkatesh, Jeff Nunn, Yi Pan, Qing Liu, Han Song, Anna Gottardi, Sanjeev Kwatra, Sanju Pancholi, Ming Cheng, Qinglang Chen, Lauren Stubel, Karthik Gopalakrishnan, Kate Bland, Raefer Gabriel, Arindam Mandal, Dilek Hakkani-Tur, Gene Hwang, Nate Michel, Eric King, and Rohit Prasad. 2018. Advancing the state of the art in open domain dialog systems through the alexa prize.

Jakub Konrád, Jan Pichl, Petr Marek, Petr Lorenc, Van Duy Ta, Ondřej Kobza, Lenka Hýlová, and Jan Šedivý. 2021. Alquist 4.0: Towards social intelligence using generative models and dialogue personalization.

Varvara Logacheva, Mikhail Burtsev, Valentin Malykh, Vadim Polulyakh, and Aleksandr Seliverstov. 2018. Convai dataset of topic-oriented human-to-chatbot dialogues. In *The NIPS'17 Competition: Building Intelligent Systems*, pages 47–57. Springer.

Douglas W. Maynard. 1980. Placement of topic changes in conversation.

M. Mori. 1970. The uncanny valley. *Energy*, 7(4):33–35.

Clifford Nass and Youngme Moon. 2000. Machines and mindlessness: Social responses to computers. *Journal of social issues*, 56(1):81–103.

Martin Porcheron, Joel E. Fischer, Stuart Reeves, and Sarah Sharples. 2018. Voice interfaces in everyday life. In *Proceedings of the 2018 CHI Conference on Human Factors in Computing Systems*, CHI '18, page 1–12, New York, NY, USA. Association for Computing Machinery.

Marek N Posard and R Gordon Rinderknecht. 2015. Do people like working with computers more than human beings? *Computers in Human Behavior*, 51:232–238.

Ashwin Ram, Rohit Prasad, Chandra Khatri, Anu Venkatesh, Raefer Gabriel, Qing Liu, Jeff Nunn, Behnam Hedayatnia, Ming Cheng, Ashish Nagar, Eric King, Kate Bland, Amanda Wartick, Yi Pan, Han Song, Sk Jayadevan, Gene Hwang, and Art Pettigrue. 2018. Conversational ai: The science behind the alexa prize.

Sougata Saha, Souvik Das, Elizabeth Soper, Erin Pacquetet, and Rohini K. Srihari. 2021. Proto: A neural cocktail for generating appealing conversations.

Weiyan Shi, Xuewei Wang, Yoo Jung Oh, Jingwen Zhang, Saurav Sahay, and Zhou Yu. 2020. Effects of persuasive dialogues: testing bot identities and inquiry strategies. In *Proceedings of the 2020 CHI Conference on Human Factors in Computing Systems*, pages 1–13.

Silvan Tomkins. 1987. Script theory. the emergence of personality. eds. joel arnoff, ai rabin, and robert a. zucker.

Sarah Theres Völkel, Daniel Buschek, Malin Eiband, Benjamin R. Cowan, and Heinrich Hussmann. 2021. Eliciting and analysing users' envisioned dialogues with perfect voice assistants. In *Proceedings of the 2021 CHI Conference on Human Factors in Computing Systems*, CHI '21, New York, NY, USA. Association for Computing Machinery.

Sarah Theres Völkel, Ramona Schödel, Daniel Buschek, Clemens Stachl, Verena Winterhalter, Markus Bühner, and Heinrich Hussmann. 2020. *Developing a Personality Model for Speech-Based Conversational Agents Using the Psycholexical Approach*, page 1–14. Association for Computing Machinery, New York, NY, USA.

Marilyn Walker, Vrindavan Harrison, Juraj Juraska, Lena Reed, Kevin Bowden, Wen Cui, Omkar Patil, and Adwait Ratnaparkhi. 2021. Athena 2.0: Contextualized dialogue management for an Alexa Prize SocialBot. In *Proceedings of the 2021 Conference* on *Empirical Methods in Natural Language Processing: System Demonstrations*, pages 124–133, Online and Punta Cana, Dominican Republic. Association for Computational Linguistics.

Terry Winograd, Fernando Flores, and Fernando F Flores. 1986. *Understanding computers and cognition: A new foundation for design*. Intellect Books.

A Appendix

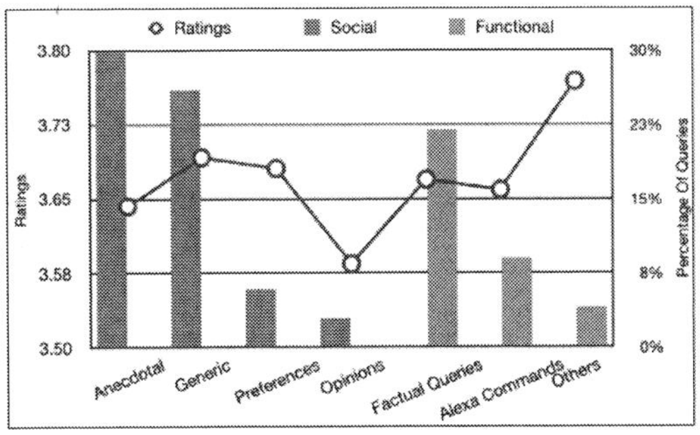

Figure 2: Analysis of different types of user queries. The primary Y-axis depicts the average rating associated with a query type across all conversations. The secondary Y-axis denotes the percentage of encountering each query.

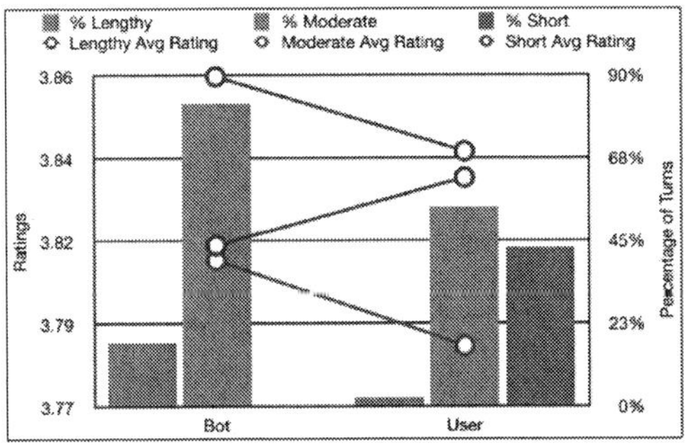

Figure 3: Analysis of bot and user response length. The primary Y-axis depicts the average rating associated with each length category across all conversations. The secondary Y-axis denotes the percentage of each length category for the bot and the user. Note that the percentage of short responses generated by the bot is very low.

Teaching Interactively to Learn Emotions in Natural Language

Rajesh Titung
Rochester Institute of Technology
New York, USA
rt7331@rit.edu

Cecilia O. Alm
Rochester Institute of Technology
New York, USA
coagla@rit.edu

Abstract

Motivated by prior literature, we provide a proof of concept simulation study for an understudied interactive machine learning method, machine teaching (MT), for the text-based emotion prediction task. We compare this method experimentally against a more well-studied technique, active learning (AL). Results show the strengths of both approaches over more resource-intensive offline supervised learning. Additionally, applying AL and MT to fine-tune a pre-trained model offers further efficiency gain. We end by recommending research directions which aim to empower users in the learning process.

1 Introduction

We examine Machine Teaching (MT), an understudied interactive machine learning (iML) method under controlled simulation for the task of *text-based emotion prediction* (Liu et al., 2003; Alm et al., 2005; Alm and Sproat, 2005; Aman and Szpakowicz, 2007; Alm, 2010; Bellegarda, 2013; Calvo and Mac Kim, 2013; Mohammad and Alm, 2015). This problem intersects with *affective computing* (Picard, 1997; Calvo et al., 2015; Poria et al., 2017), and a family of language inference problems characterized by human *subjectivity* in learning targets (Alm, 2011) and semantic-pragmatic meaning (Wiebe et al., 2004). Both subjectivity and the lack of data for learning to recognize affective states motivate iML techniques. Here, we focus on resource efficiency. Our findings from simulations provide directions for user experiments.

Human perception - and thus human annotators' interpretation - is influenced by human factors such as preferences, cultural differences, bias, domain expertise, fatigue, time on task, or mood at annotation time (Alm, 2012; Amidei et al., 2020; Shen and Rose, 2021). Generally, experts with long-standing practice or in-depth knowledge may also not share consensus (Plank et al., 2014). Inter-subjective

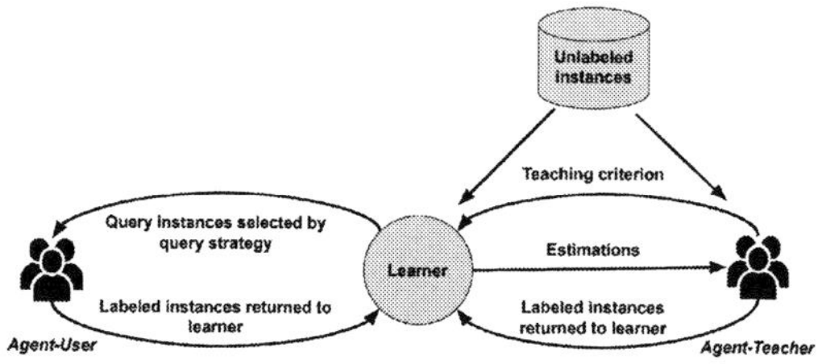

Figure 1: Comparison of interactive *Active Learning* (left) with *Machine Teaching* (right). Training instances are labeled by the Agent-User (in AL) or the Agent-Teacher (in MT).

disagreements can reflect invalid noise artifact (detectable by humans) or *ecologically valid* differences in interpretation.

Holzinger (2016) define iML methods as algorithmic procedures that "*can interact with agents and can optimize their learning behavior through these interactions* [...]" (p. 119). In our study, the stakeholders in the learning process are models (*learners*) and humans (*agent-users* or *agent-teachers*). Tegen et al. (2020) posit that iML involves either *Active Learning* (AL) or interactive *Machine Teaching* (MT),[1] based on humans' role in the learning loop. In AL, the learning algorithm uses *query strategies* (e.g., triggered by *uncertainty*) to iteratively select instances from which it learns (Settles, 2009) if licensed by a *budget*; with a human agent who annotates upon learner request. In contrast, in MT, the teacher (user) who possesses problem knowledge instead selects the instances to be labeled and uses them to train the learner (Zhu, 2015). Initial, foundational MT research focused on constructing a minimal, ideal set of training data, striving for optimality in the data the learner is presented with to learn from. Interactive MT assumes human agent interaction with the learner (Liu et al., 2017), for enabling time- and resource-efficient

[1] We use conventions from Tegen et al. (2020) where MT means an iterative, interactive implementation of Machine Teaching. MT here is not Machine Translation.

Proceedings of the Second Workshop on Bridging Human–Computer Interaction and Natural Language Processing, pages 40 - 46
July 15, 2022

model convergence. Following the training by error criterion described in Tegen et al. (2020), if the learner is unable to predict the right answer, and the budget allows, the human teacher instructs the learner with the label. Thus, AL leverages measures to wisely choose instances for human labeling and subsequent learning, whereas MT capitalizes on the teacher's knowledge to wisely select training instances and proceed to learn when the criterion to teach is met (cf. Figure 1).

2 Related Work and Background

Olsson (2009) discussed AL for NLP tasks, while Schröder and Niekler (2020) discussed deep learning with AL. Our study also builds on Tegen et al. (2020)'s use of simulation to study AL query strategies and MT assessment and teaching criteria. Lu and MacNamee (2020) reported on experiments where transformer-based representations performed consistently better than other text representations, taking advantage of the label information that arises in AL. An et al. (2018) also suggested assigning a varying number of instances to label per human oracle based on their capability/skills and the amount of unlabeled data, which reduced the time required by the deep learner without negatively impacting performance. We comparatively study iML in the fine-tuning stages. Bai et al. (2020) emphasized language-based attributes like reconstruction of word-based cross-entropy loss across words in sentences toward instance selection. To ensure improved experimental control and avoid confounding variables, we focus on uncertainty-based strategies for AL.

MT deals with a teacher designing a well-reasoned, ideally optimal, training set to drive the learner to the desired target concept/model (Zhu, 2015; Zhu et al., 2018). While there has been some progress in the use of MT, its application in NLP is present in its earliest form with little empirical exploration or refinement. MT has been explored mostly in computing security, where the teacher is a *hacker/advisor* who selects training data to adjust the behavior of an adaptive, evolving learner (Alfeld et al., 2016, 2017). Tegen et al. (2020) reported that MT could greatly reduce the number of instances required, and even outperformed most AL strategies. These findings are compelling and motivate exploring MT's potential in NLP, which, however, has some distinct characteristics, including high-dimensional data impacted by scarcity. MT's possibilities in NLP are thus as of yet largely unknown. We begin here by focusing on controlled experimental simulations to examine resource-efficiency and performance in text-based emotion prediction, whereas future work will take a step closer to ecological validity in interactive MT with real-time agent-teachers.

Overall, several prospects can be noted for NLP with interactive Machine Learning (iML):

- Human knowledge and insights can be leveraged to make the *search space substantially smaller* by systematic instance selection (Holzinger, 2016), achieving adequate performance with fewer training instances.
- In a setting where learning occurs online or continually (Tegen et al., 2019), iML enables *sustained learning* over time, with new or updated data offered to the learner. This especially makes sense for natural language tasks which by nature are characterized by linguistic change.
- Using iML can enable model *customization* to specific users, schools of thought, and enable privacy-preserving models (Bernardo et al., 2017), e.g., for deploying NLP on edge devices.
- IML enables users to directly influence the model (Amershi et al., 2014), and interactive techniques can aid agents to *catch bias or concept drift early* in the development process.
- The iML paradigm enables an *initial state with limited data* (or even a *cold start*), which applies to NLP for underresourced languages, low-data clinical problems, etc., including NLP for affective computing since many affective states remain understudied (Alm, n.d.).
- By learning more resource-efficiently, iML has potential to *lower NLP's carbon footprint*.

While iML is promising, issues include:

- Humans users or teachers are *not necessarily willing or available* to provide input or feedback to a system (Donmez and Carbonell, 2010).
- The iML setup is not immune to *catastrophic forgetting* (Holzinger, 2016) in online learning.
- Human factors introduce technical considerations that may impact interaction and performance success; for instance, the learning set-up should accommodate *human fatigue* (Darani and Kaedi, 2017; Llorà et al., 2005).

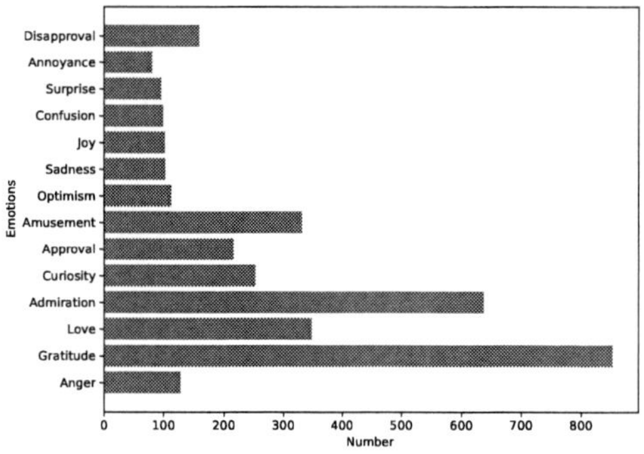

Figure 2: Class imbalance for the 14-class emotion data.

3 MT/AL for Emotion Prediction

Text-based emotion data are subject to variation and ambiguity, which adds to the difficulty in the annotation process, compounded with data scarcity for capturing many affective states. IML methods can be a means to deal with data limitations.

In this study, we used a subset of the GoEmotions dataset (Demszky et al., 2020) which consists of emotion labels for Reddit comments. We prioritized resource-efficiency as the primary experimental variable over exploring impact on target concept ambiguity. Figure 2 shows the imbalanced distribution of emotion classes in this subset. The training and test sets comprised approximately 2800 and 700 instances respectively. In all experiments, the learner was trained initially with 10% of the training set while the remaining 90% was reserved as an unlabeled pool of data which were gradually added to the training set in each iteration.[2] The simulated 'user' had access to the labels of the instances from the unlabeled dataset whenever required via dataset lookup.

3.1 AL vs. MT for Emotion Prediction

We compared the effect of AL and MT strategies and further compared to offline supervised machine learning, referred to as *all-in-one batch*.

Motivation In our AL experiment, the learner queried the instances using versions of *uncertainty sampling* or a *random* approach. In the *least confident* strategy, the learner selects instances for query for which it has the least probability of prediction in its most probable class; in *margin sampling*, instances with the smallest difference between its top-two most likely classes; and in *entropy*, with the largest entropy (Olsson, 2009; Tegen et al., 2020).

In MT, the agent-teacher chooses instances (Zhu, 2015), which are then labeled and used to teach the learner (Tegen et al., 2020). We simulated the *margin sampling*-based AL query strategy as a teacher to select a set of instances. Moreover, *error-based* and *state change* are two *teaching criteria* used by Tegen et al. (2020) for initiating teaching. In the error-based method, the teacher proceeds to teach based on correctness of the learner's estimation, i.e., supplying the learner with the correct label for wrong estimations. We introduce a modification termed *error-based training with counting* where the teacher continues to provide labeled instances to the learner when all estimations are accurate in two consecutive iterations to ensure periodic model updating. In the state change-based criterion, the teacher provides a label for the instance if the current instance's real class label differs from the prior instance's class label. When no label is given, the learner assumes the instance's label is the same as the last label given by the teacher.

Methods We focus on transportability and opted for sklearn's Linear SVM with hinge loss given its lean computational character (Buitinck et al., 2013; Chang and Lin, 2011). Both setups were trained on CPUs, with MT using state change as teaching criterion taking the longest time (around 40 min).

Results and Discussion Panel (a) in Figure 3 shows the result for AL strategies. The performance on emotion prediction in text is more resource-efficient and uses less data with AL. The query strategies achieved the performance equivalent to learning with the full batch of training data after using just around half of the data with AL, and all perform better than random selection. A Wilcoxon's Rank Sum Test (Wilcoxon, 1992) for independent samples compared random against other query strategies. This indicated a significant difference in their performance with $p < 0.05$. Panel (b) shows the MT results for three teaching criteria. State change improves over the error-based approach, while the error-based approach with counting slightly enhances the regular error-based approach because of the modification introduced. We also observe that since we used margin-based AL

[2]For the Huggingface transformers library 20% of the training set was held out as a validation set before this 90-10 split. For sklearn, attempts at hyperparameter tuning–for the C parameter, dual/primal problem and tolerance values for stopping criteria–used a genetic algorithm without meaningful performance difference, and results are provided with defaults, with class weights initiated as the inverse of the frequency of each class.

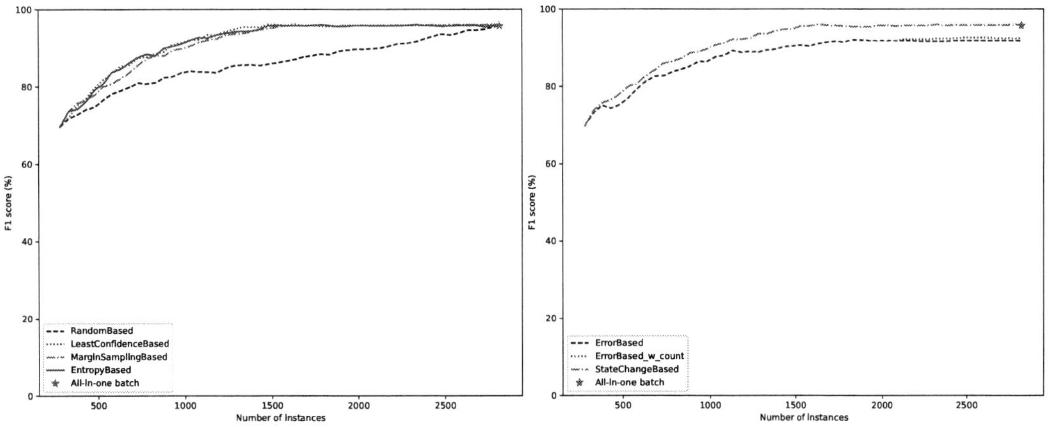

(a) AL query strategies

(b) MT teaching criteria

Figure 3: Text-based emotion prediction with (a) AL query strategies or (b) MT teaching criteria. The all-in-one batch option (green star) signifies resource-inefficient offline batch training.

as a teacher for selecting instances, the result mirrors margin sampling-based AL in panel (a). Moreover, we note that error-based teaching saturates, potentially reflecting that state change-based teaching is more capable of dealing with imbalanced data (Tegen et al., 2020). Overall, the encouraging results motivate us to plan to assess utility in a real-time MT scenario with a human teacher and deeper study of teacher variations for data selection and revised teaching criteria for initiating training.

3.2 Fine-tuning with AL and MT

Motivation Previous results showed that MT and AL can build better models more efficiently with annotation savings (time and cost). Here, we explore if fine-tuning a pre-trained model – a frequent and often performance-boosting approach in NLP – that uses iML concepts can improve results further.

Methods We fine-tune a pre-trained BERT model (Devlin et al., 2019) to emotion prediction in text using Huggingface (Wolf et al., 2020), with a max. sequence length of 80 (since comments tend to be quite short). Based on prior observations, we analyze fine-tuning performance with AL for the least confident and margin sampling strategies, and with MT for the error-based and error-based with counting teaching criteria.

Results and Discussion Figure 4 shows the outcomes for fine-tuning BERT interactively. The results show performance close to 96%, which is good for this subjective task. Moreover, AL matched the offline training performance using less than half of the available instances. We note that convergence for fine-tuning also required somewhat less data than in the prior SVM-based experiment, as shown by the steeper slope of performance increment. Yet how to better leverage MT in conjunction with fine-tuning, or transfer techniques generally, remains a key priority in continued study.

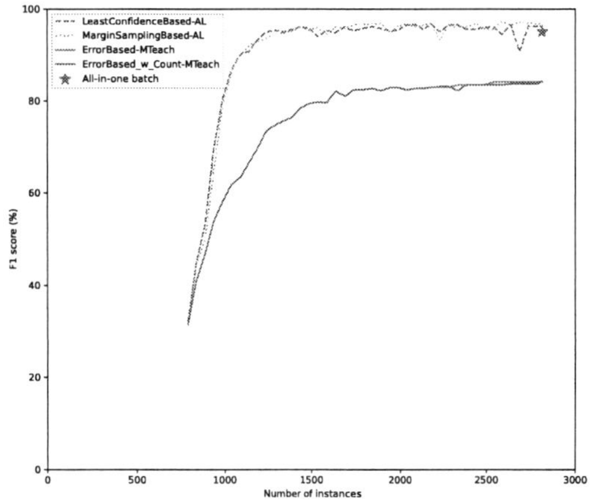

Figure 4: Text-based emotion prediction when using AL or MT in fine-tuning with BERT.

4 Discussion

We showed that iML efficiently produces desired results for text-based emotion prediction. MT remains understudied and should be further explored for NLP tasks. Fine-tuning a pre-trained model with AL can leverage the strengths of both approaches with small datasets. In addition to experiments detailed above, we explored training the learner *incrementally* (online training) versus in a *non-incremental* setup (the learner is trained using accumulated training set up to the most recent query). The incremental approach experiences *catastrophic forgetting* but requires very little time for learner updating and can thus work well under low memory usage, e.g., for a life-long learning setting or edge devices.

5 Conclusion

Our study on text-based emotion prediction demonstrated the potential of both MT and AL methods. We offered initial experimentation with MT and AL for this problem, and based on promising results under controlled simulation, next steps will focus on real-time user/teacher interactions, a broader set of teaching criteria, and new forms of training instance selection. In addition, we are interested in exploring heavily understudied affective states, which are currently not covered sufficiently or not covered at all in annotated emotion corpora. We also suggest focused research on specialized teachers in NLP tasks toward better selection of training data. Teachers who assess the learner and decide the right time to offer an adequate set of new information may also help create more robust or interpretable learners which evolve over time.

Ethics Statement

A limitation of this work is that it did not consider linguistic characteristics of the pre-trained models (Bai et al., 2020). We used an artificial teacher in MT and did not deeply examine hybrid MT-AL strategies, although we used an AL approach as teacher in the MT setup. Still, this work may stimulate NLP researchers to consider the benefits of AL and MT, especially for challenging subjective NLP tasks such as text-based emotion prediction (Alm, 2011). Additionally, continued work can explore how the findings apply in the context of other corpora, including with multimodal data.

Acknowledgements

This material is based upon work supported by the National Science Foundation under Award No. DGE-2125362. Any opinions, findings, and conclusions or recommendations expressed in this material are those of the author(s) and do not necessarily reflect the views of the National Science Foundation.

References

Scott Alfeld, Xiaojin Zhu, and Paul Barford. 2016. Data poisoning attacks against autoregressive models. In *Proceedings of the Thirtieth AAAI Conference on Artificial Intelligence*, AAAI'16, page 1452–1458. AAAI Press.

Scott Alfeld, Xiaojin Zhu, and Paul Barford. 2017. Explicit defense actions against test-set attacks. In *Proceedings of the Thirty-First AAAI Conference on Artificial Intelligence*, AAAI'17, page 1274–1280. AAAI Press.

Cecilia Ovesdotter Alm. 2010. Characteristics of high agreement affect annotation in text. In *Proceedings of the Fourth Linguistic Annotation Workshop*, pages 118–122, Uppsala, Sweden. Association for Computational Linguistics.

Cecilia Ovesdotter Alm. 2011. Subjective natural language problems: Motivations, applications, characterizations, and implications. In *Proceedings of the 49th Annual Meeting of the Association for Computational Linguistics: Human Language Technologies: short papers-Volume 2*, pages 107–112. Association for Computational Linguistics.

Cecilia Ovesdotter Alm. 2012. The role of affect in the computational modeling of natural language. *Language and Linguistics Compass*, 6(7):416–430.

Cecilia Ovesdotter Alm. n.d. Linguistic data resources for computational emotion sensing and modeling.

Cecilia Ovesdotter Alm, Dan Roth, and Richard Sproat. 2005. Emotions from text: Machine learning for text-based emotion prediction. In *Proceedings of Human Language Technology Conference and Conference on Empirical Methods in Natural Language Processing*, pages 579–586, Vancouver, British Columbia, Canada. Association for Computational Linguistics.

Cecilia Ovesdotter Alm and Richard Sproat. 2005. Emotional sequencing and development in fairy tales. In *Affective Computing and Intelligent Interaction*, pages 668–674, Berlin, Heidelberg. Springer Berlin Heidelberg.

Saima Aman and Stan Szpakowicz. 2007. Identifying expressions of emotion in text. In Mautner P. Matoušek V., editor, *Text, Speech and Dialogue TSD 2007*, pages 196–205. Springer.

Saleema Amershi, Maya Cakmak, William Bradley Knox, and Todd Kulesza. 2014. Power to the people: The role of humans in interactive machine learning. *AI Magazine*, 35(4):105–120.

Jacopo Amidei, Paul Piwek, and Alistair Willis. 2020. Identifying annotator bias: A new IRT-based method for bias identification. In *Proceedings of the 28th International Conference on Computational Linguistics*, pages 4787–4797, Barcelona, Spain (Online). International Committee on Computational Linguistics.

Bang An, Wenjun Wu, and Huimin Han. 2018. Deep active learning for text classification. In *Proceedings of the 2nd International Conference on Vision, Image and Signal Processing*, ICVISP 2018, New York, NY, USA. Association for Computing Machinery.

Guirong Bai, Shizhu He, Kang Liu, Jun Zhao, and Zaiqing Nie. 2020. Pre-trained language model based active learning for sentence matching. In *Proceedings of the 28th International Conference on Computational Linguistics*, pages 1495–1504, Barcelona, Spain (Online). International Committee on Computational Linguistics.

Jerome R. Bellegarda. 2013. Data-driven analysis of emotion in text using latent affective folding and embedding. *Computational Intelligence*, 29(3):506–526.

Francisco Bernardo, Michael Zbyszynski, Rebecca Fiebrink, and Mick Grierson. 2017. Interactive machine learning for end-user innovation. In *AAAI Spring Symposia*, pages 369–375.

Lars Buitinck, Gilles Louppe, Mathieu Blondel, Fabian Pedregosa, Andreas Mueller, Olivier Grisel, Vlad Niculae, Peter Prettenhofer, Alexandre Gramfort, Jaques Grobler, Robert Layton, Jake VanderPlas, Arnaud Joly, Brian Holt, and Gaël Varoquaux. 2013. API design for machine learning software: Experiences from the scikit-learn project. In *ECML PKDD Workshop: Languages for Data Mining and Machine Learning*, pages 108–122.

Rafael Calvo, Sidney D'Mello, Jonathan Gratch, and Arvid Kappas, editors. 2015. *The Oxford Handbook of Affective Computing*. Oxford University Press.

Rafael A. Calvo and Sunghwan Mac Kim. 2013. Emotions in text: Dimensional and categorical models. *Computational Intelligence*, 29(3):527–543.

Chih-Chung Chang and Chih-Jen Lin. 2011. LIBSVM: A library for support vector machines. *ACM Transactions on Intelligent Systems and Technology*, 2:27:1–27:27. Software available at `http://www.csie.ntu.edu.tw/~cjlin/libsvm`.

Zahra Sheikhi Darani and Marjan Kaedi. 2017. Improving the interactive genetic algorithm for customer-centric product design by automatically scoring the unfavorable designs. *Human-centeric Computing and Information Sciences*, 7(38).

Dorottya Demszky, Dana Movshovitz-Attias, Jeongwoo Ko, Alan Cowen, Gaurav Nemade, and Sujith Ravi. 2020. GoEmotions: A dataset of fine-grained emotions. In *Proceedings of the 58th Annual Meeting of the Association for Computational Linguistics"*, pages 4040–4054, Online. Association for Computational Linguistics.

Jacob Devlin, Ming-Wei Chang, Kenton Lee, and Kristina Toutanova. 2019. BERT: Pre-training of deep bidirectional transformers for language understanding. In *Proceedings of the 2019 Conference of the North American Chapter of the Association for Computational Linguistics: Human Language Technologies, Volume 1 (Long and Short Papers)*, pages 4171–4186, Minneapolis, Minnesota. Association for Computational Linguistics.

Pinar Donmez and Jaime Carbonell. 2010. *From Active to Proactive Learning Methods*, volume 262, pages 97–120. Springer Berlin Heidelberg.

Andreas Holzinger. 2016. Interactive machine learning for health informatics: when do we need the human-in-the-loop? *Brain Informatics*, 3(2):119–131.

Hugo Liu, Henry Lieberman, and Ted Selker. 2003. A model of textual affect sensing using real-world knowledge. In *Proceedings of the 8th International Conference on Intelligent User Interfaces*, IUI '03, page 125–132, New York, NY, USA. Association for Computing Machinery.

Weiyang Liu, Bo Dai, Ahmad Humayun, Charlene Tay, Chen Yu, Linda B. Smith, James M. Rehg, and Le Song. 2017. Iterative machine teaching. In *Proceedings of the 34th International Conference on Machine Learning - Volume 70*, ICML'17, page 2149–2158. JMLR.org.

Xavier Llorà, Kumara Sastry, David E. Goldberg, Abhimanyu Gupta, and Lalitha Lakshmi. 2005. Combating user fatigue in IGAs: Partial ordering, support vector machines, and synthetic fitness. In *Proceedings of the 7th Annual Conference on Genetic and Evolutionary Computation*, GECCO '05, page 1363–1370, New York, NY, USA. Association for Computing Machinery.

Jinghui Lu and Brian MacNamee. 2020. Investigating the effectiveness of representations based on pretrained transformer-based language models in active learning for labelling text datasets. *arXiv e-prints*, page arXiv:2004.13138.

Saif Mohammad and Cecilia O. Alm. 2015. Computational analysis of affect and emotion in language. In *Proceedings of the 2015 Conference on Empirical Methods in Natural Language Processing: Tutorial Abstracts*, Lisbon, Portugal. Association for Computational Linguistics.

Fredrik Olsson. 2009. A literature survey of active machine learning in the context of natural language processing. Technical report, Swedish Institute of Computer Science.

Rosalind W. Picard. 1997. *Affective Computing*. MIT Press, Cambridge, MA.

Barbara Plank, Dirk Hovy, and Anders Søgaard. 2014. Linguistically debatable or just plain wrong? In *Proceedings of the 52nd Annual Meeting of the Association for Computational Linguistics (Volume 2: Short Papers)*, pages 507–511, Baltimore, Maryland. Association for Computational Linguistics.

Soujanya Poria, Erik Cambria, Rajiv Bajpai, and Amir Hussain. 2017. A review of affective computing: From unimodal analysis to multimodal fusion. *Information Fusion*, 37:98 – 125.

Christopher Schröder and Andreas Niekler. 2020. A survey of active learning for text classification using deep neural networks. *arXiv*, 2008.07267.

Burr Settles. 2009. Active learning literature survey. Computer Sciences Technical Report 1648, University of Wisconsin–Madison.

Qinlan Shen and Carolyn Rose. 2021. What sounds "right" to me? Experiential factors in the perception of political ideology. In *Proceedings of the 16th Conference of the European Chapter of the Association for Computational Linguistics: Main Volume*, pages 1762–1771, Online. Association for Computational Linguistics.

Agnes Tegen, Paul Davidsson, and Jan A. Persson. 2019. Towards a taxonomy of interactive continual and multimodal learning for the internet of things. In *Adjunct Proceedings of the 2019 ACM International Joint Conference on Pervasive and Ubiquitous Computing and Proceedings of the 2019 ACM International Symposium on Wearable Computers*, UbiComp/ISWC '19 Adjunct, page 524–528, New York, NY, USA. Association for Computing Machinery.

Agnes Tegen, Paul Davidsson, and Jan A. Persson. 2020. A taxonomy of interactive online machine learning strategies. In *Machine Learning and Knowledge Discovery in Databases - European Conference, ECML PKDD 2020, Ghent, Belgium, September 14-18, 2020, Proceedings, Part II*, volume 12458 of *Lecture Notes in Computer Science*, pages 137–153. Springer.

Janyce Wiebe, Theresa Wilson, Rebecca Bruce, Matthew Bell, and Melanie Martin. 2004. Learning subjective language. *Computational Linguistics*, 30(3):277–308.

Frank Wilcoxon. 1992. Individual comparisons by ranking methods. In Samuel Kotz and Norman L. Johnson, editors, *Breakthroughs in Statistics: Methodology and Distribution*, pages 196–202. Springer New York, New York, NY.

Thomas Wolf, Lysandre Debut, Victor Sanh, Julien Chaumond, Clement Delangue, Anthony Moi, Pierric Cistac, Tim Rault, Remi Louf, Morgan Funtowicz, Joe Davison, Sam Shleifer, Patrick von Platen, Clara Ma, Yacine Jernite, Julien Plu, Canwen Xu, Teven Le Scao, Sylvain Gugger, Mariama Drame, Quentin Lhoest, and Alexander Rush. 2020. Transformers: State-of-the-art natural language processing. In *Proceedings of the 2020 Conference on Empirical Methods in Natural Language Processing: System Demonstrations*, pages 38–45, Online. Association for Computational Linguistics.

Xiaojin Zhu. 2015. Machine teaching: An inverse problem to machine learning and an approach toward optimal education. *Proceedings of the AAAI Conference on Artificial Intelligence*, 29(1).

Xiaojin Zhu, Adish Singla, Sandra Zilles, and Anna N. Rafferty. 2018. An overview of machine teaching. *CoRR*, abs/1801.05927.

Narrative Datasets through the Lenses of NLP and HCI

Sharifa Sultana
Cornell University
ss3634@cornell.edu

Renwen Zhang
National University of Singapore
r.zhang@nus.edu.sg

Hajin Lim
Seoul National University
hajin@snu.ac.kr

Maria Antoniak
Cornell University
maa343@cornell.edu

Abstract

In this short paper, we compare existing value systems and approaches in NLP and HCI for collecting narrative data. Building on these parallel discussions, we shed light on the challenges facing some popular NLP dataset types, which we discuss these in relation to widely-used narrative-based HCI research methods; and we highlight points where NLP methods can broaden qualitative narrative studies. In particular, we point towards contextuality, positionality, dataset size, and open research design as central points of difference and windows for collaboration when studying narratives. Through the use case of narratives, this work contributes to a larger conversation regarding the possibilities for bridging NLP and HCI through speculative mixed-methods.

1 Introduction

Human beings are myth-makers; we use stories and imagination to create communities and make sense of the world and our place in it (Bamberg and Georgakopoulou, 2008). Narratives are powerful modes of expression, with physical, emotional, and social benefits for both the narrator and the audience (Pennebaker and Beall, 1986; Pennebaker, 1997; Merz et al., 2014; Oh and Kim, 2016; Tangherlini, 2000). They can also be powerful methods for understanding human behavior and beliefs (Golsteijn and Wright, 2013).

Crucially, narratives are *situated*; they are told and take place in specific social contexts (Piper et al., 2021). Natural language processing (NLP) methods can analyze patterns across large datasets, putting stories into context. But narrative datasets in NLP are often removed from the narratives' original contexts (e.g., scraped internet datasets) or are designed without any explicit context or social grounding (e.g., short and artificial stories).

In contrast, contextuality is of the utmost importance in qualitative human-computer interaction (HCI) approaches to narrative. HCI researchers frequently borrow social science methods including surveys, interviews, focus groups, and ethnography for closer investigations that address the diversity of human life and experiences (Bruner, 1987; Golsteijn and Wright, 2013). Qualitative HCI methods are often constrained to small sample sizes and susceptible to observer biases, but narrative research and portraiture methods enable creative and holistic engagement with participants' experiences and meaning-making processes (Williams, 1984; Wright and McCarthy, 2004; Bardzell et al., 2012).

These differences make narrative datasets an useful case study when considering tensions and possible collaborations between NLP and HCI. Both disciplines face challenges in their study and analysis of narrative. While NLP datasets contain a high volume of data points, their labels are constrained to a specific task; in contrast, smaller HCI datasets, in particular data collected through qualitative methods such as ethnography and interview, are open-ended in research scope but situated in a particular context. Combining these methods can contribute to designing multifaceted datasets while not losing the sight of individual experiences and perspectives in a large volume of stories.

In the following sections, we outline dominant framings of narrative and narrative dataset collection in NLP and HCI. Placing these framings side-by-side highlights a set of tensions—including dataset size, contextuality and positionality, and dataset design—that we finally consider as material for synthesis and mixed methods approaches to narrative data.

2 NLP Framings of Narrative

In a recent overview of NLP and humanist approaches to "narrative understanding", Piper et al. (2021) formulate narrativity as a scalar construct rather than a binary class; texts can include some or all narrative features (e.g., narrator, audience, se-

Proceedings of the Second Workshop on Bridging Human–Computer Interaction and Natural Language Processing, pages 47 - 54
July 15, 2022 ©2022 Association for Computational Linguistics

quential actions). Most NLP narrative tasks focus on building **abstractions** from narratives by extracting these features and measuring relationships among them. These tasks include extracting narrative **structure**, like scripts, plot units, or narrative arcs (Schank and Abelson, 1977; Lehnert, 1981; Chambers and Jurafsky, 2008, 2009; Goyal et al., 2010; Reagan et al., 2016); modeling **connections** between characters (Bamman et al., 2013; Iyyer et al., 2016; Lukin et al., 2016); **generating** new stories or summaries (Goldfarb-Tarrant et al., 2020; Guan et al., 2020; Akoury et al., 2020); answering **questions** about the story (Richardson et al., 2013), and identifying a correct story **ending** (Chambers and Jurafsky, 2008; Mostafazadeh et al., 2016).

As in other areas of NLP, some narrative research falls into *shared tasks*, where **artificial** story datasets are often (though not always) used for testing a particular technical ability of a system. These datasets are sometimes created and often labeled by crowdworkers, and they include brief scenarios not explicitly connected to broader social contexts and narratives. For example, one of the widely used corpora for testing performance on the Story Cloze task is ROCStories dataset which is a collection of 100,000 crowdsourced "five-sentence commonsense stories" (Mostafazadeh et al., 2016).

Narrative research in NLP also includes *corpus-based* studies, where researchers use narrative models to learn about a particular dataset and its authors. Corpus-based studies depend on **curated** datasets that range widely, e.g., fictional works (e.g., novels, fairytales) (Jans et al., 2012; Iyyer et al., 2016), news stories (Chambers and Jurafsky, 2008), biographies (Bamman and Smith, 2014), and personal stories shared orally or on social media (Gordon and Swanson, 2009; Ouyang and McKeown, 2014; Antoniak et al., 2019). These curated datasets were authored in social contexts separate from the NLP research study and are gathered afterwards. Curated datasets can also be used for shared tasks, e.g., coreference resolution (Bamman et al., 2020), story generation (Akoury et al., 2020).

There are a small number of **naturalistic** NLP narrative datasets that lie outside of the above categories. For example, Sap et al. (2020) collected autobiographical stories and retellings of these stories from crowdworkers; this data was shared as part of the research study but was also grounded in the authors' personal experiences.

And finally, many modern NLP methods for narratives rely on large, pretrained models (Devlin et al., 2019). These models are trained on **massive** and (mostly) undocumented datasets, containing a mixture of documents from unrelated domains to generalize to other domains and tasks (after fine-tuning). These pretraining datasets, like the aptly-named Pile (Gao et al., 2020), are too large for full datasheet descriptions (Gebru et al., 2021) and can encode human biases (Bender et al., 2021).

3 HCI Framings of Narrative

Four key themes are associated with HCI's sensibility of narrative: (a) fact (universal/objective truth) (b) experience (global, local, and day-to-day experiences) (c) interpretation (perceived understanding of a and b) (d) fiction (imaginations and cultural value-system based storytelling) (Bruner, 1990; Sterling, 2009; Golsteijn and Wright, 2013). HCI researchers often ask questions to understand problems better and care about accuracy, legitimacy, and materiality (i.e., why and how certain issues are important) of information. Many subdomains of HCI refer to and build on users' experiences regarding narratives (Feuston and Piper, 2019). HCI practitioners' and designers' interactions with social settings and/or professional environments frequently influence their experiences in a given time and situation, and so they consciously refrain from making generalizable statements and encourage the mention of **contextuality**, which is strongly associated with the narratives (Golsteijn and Wright, 2013). Experience-centered research also values **empathy** to understand the researchers' orientation to the user, and whether they are motivated to empathize with the users' needs and emotional responses (Wright and McCarthy, 2008).

HCI uses both qualitative and quantitative techniques to gather and examine narratives. Both quantitative techniques (e.g., surveys and computational analysis of social media data) and qualitative approaches (e.g., interviews, observation, and focus groups) and artistic techniques are frequent in HCI. In this paper, we focus on qualitative HCI methods for narratives, as they differ from NLP approaches in terms of ontology and epistemology, representing two distinct worldviews (Slevitch, 2011).

In **surveys**, researchers conduct statistical analyses and evaluate the responses based on standard tests and sets of metrics. Using qualitative text coding in cases of free-text responses within the survey is also common. More specifically, HCI scholars have conducted surveys to investigate people's motivations, goals, and challenges with regard to posting narratives on social media (Sannon et al., 2019), as well as factors that influence their decision-making when it comes to online disclosure (Bazarova et al., 2015; Zhang et al., 2021) These approaches are motivated by understanding a specific set of people in a specific setting and social context.

Ethnography, observations, interviews, focus group discussions, and story-telling are common methods used by qualitative HCI researchers (Sultana and Ahmed, 2019). Other than transcription-based qualitative text coding, image, audio and video coding are also used for analysis (Andalibi et al., 2017; Sharma and De Choudhury, 2015). In this regard, not only the texts, images, audio, and videos of the participants are used, but also pictures of the environment, background noise, and even reasons and results of unintended interruptions can contribute to the richness of narratives.

HCI researchers also use curated **social media data** and conduct statistical analyses and qualitative text coding on this data to understand certain research problems. HCI researchers in some domains also use online ethnographic techniques on social media and collaborative platforms (e.g., gaming, e-commerce) to grow deeper understandings of these communities (Mim and Ahmed, 2020).

Many HCI researchers and participants use **artistic techniques** like drawings and installations for addressing research queries (Sturdee et al., 2021). It is quite common for artists to conduct an auto-ethnography with themselves, in which their creation of art is their narrative. In many cases, such narratives are symbolic and contextual.

Finally, many HCI researchers adopt **mixed methods** where they use both qualitative and quantitative approaches to grow a wider and deeper understanding of their research problems. For example, a recent feminist-HCI design used a survey to understand the spread of gender harassment on social media and also conducted interviews and focus group discussions for participatory design and user evaluation of *Unmochon* (Sultana et al., 2021).

4 Interdisciplinary Tensions

Volume and depth of narratives. On one hand, NLP techniques can analyze more narratives (and often more normalized) with reduced researcher workload, though at the loss of qualitative detail. On the other hand, qualitative methods in HCI offer a deeper understanding of narratives based on a more limited sample size. Despite smaller datasets, HCI often depends on theoretical saturation of narratives, in which all important themes are represented, while in NLP, even if the number of datapoints is greater, researchers interested in a particular community often rely on an extracted sample decided by someone else (i.e., *curated* datasets) which might not capture all relevant themes.

4.1 Abstraction and Contextuality

While gaining holistic understandings of an individual in HCI, researchers care about participants' life experiences, social relationships, and observable artifacts surrounding them. In NLP research, it is often impossible to glean such relevant and detailed information from individuals in a large dataset, where abstraction rather than situatedness is the goal. This contrast also pertains to the *agency and privacy* of the narrative sources—whether authors are informed about and consent to the inclusion of their narrative in the dataset for research purposes—as well as the uncertain *representation* of different groups. Narrative data in NLP often lacks explicit context (artificial datasets) or is used out of context (curated and massive datasets); naturalistic datasets generated specifically for the NLP study are more rare (Sap et al., 2020), unlike in HCI. For example, it is common in NLP to scrape data passively that was written in a different context than the research study, as opposed to interview studies in HCI, where researchers explicitly collect stories for the current study. However, NLP datasets are often designed tasks that model abstractions, like common narrative arcs, where simplified datasets can help researchers tackle specific tasks.

4.2 Closed and Open Dataset Design.

HCI's emphasis on contextuality opens rather than constrains research possibilities: when narratives are collected in HCI, the emphasis is on high-level and open-ended research goals, focusing on discovering things that have not been explored sufficiently or that might even be in conflict with the researchers' assumptions. Similarly, when labeling themes in narratives, multiple HCI researchers are involved in an open coding process, in which independent coders develop their own themes before combining and refining these themes to ensure the validity and reliability of their interpretations. In contrast, shared narrative tasks in NLP rely on labeled datasets intended for one task, whose data and labels are meant to model one specific concept (like story conclusions) that the researchers already hold, even if multiple annotators are involved.

5 Towards a Mixed Methods Approach

We argue that mixed methods research, drawing from both NLP and HCI, could allow for richer narrative datasets and more holistic understandings of narrative and the social impacts of narrative. This *triangulation* of methods not only minimizes the biases of researchers and enhances the validity of the findings, but also reveals different dimensions of the phenomenon being investigated (McQueen and Knussen, 2002). While prior work has suggested mixed methods in many other NLP contexts (e.g., grounded topic modeling (Baumer et al., 2017)), narratives are particularly well-suited because of the strong research interest on both sides and the tensions enumerated above.

5.1 Customizing an Approach

Prior work has suggested various frameworks to select between mixed methods approaches (Heuer and Buschek, 2021; Inie and Derczynski, 2021). These mixed methods may follow different design patterns, including *explanatory*, *exploratory*, *parallel*, and *nested* methods (Creswell and Clark, 2017). Therefore, the choice of study design should be guided by research questions and goals. For example, if researchers aim to understand the structural patterns of a certain type of narrative (e.g., mental health disclosures on social media) and examine its situatedness (i.e., audiences and context), they might consider an explanatory sequential mixed methods design, where researchers first use quantitative methods to analyze scraped data followed by qualitative interviews and selected narratives in social context. Contrarily, to understand how individuals frame a particular event or phenomenon (e.g., the COVID-19 pandemic) and see if that frame can be applied to a larger population, researchers might opt for an exploratory sequential mixed methods design, characterized by an initial qualitative phase of data collection and analysis, followed by quantitative analysis drawing on a larger dataset.

5.2 Contextuality

Because situatedness or contextuality are essential components of narrative, contextuality can act as a bridging frame in these mixed methods designs, to move between the volume of narrative data in NLP and the depth of analysis in qualitative HCI methods. Researchers can move between "zooming in" on specific stories using qualitative methods and "zooming out" to analyze larger patterns across stories (rather than just one or the other). For example, HCI methods can be used to gather qualitative detail about a dataset's context, while research methods and tools from NLP can help HCI researchers situate smaller datasets within their larger-scale, cross-community contexts (Zhang et al., 2017; Lucy and Bamman, 2021). Both sets of methods can also help address how platform design, moderation, and other contextual features shape the sharing of narratives online.

5.3 Positionality in Design and Evaluation.

Qualitative HCI methods emphasize reflexivity and positionality. These practices can encourage NLP researchers to recognize the inherent biases in their research questions, datasets, modeling architectures, procedures, and interpretation of results. Narrative tasks are not simple; each instance usually has multiple right answers, and researchers need to be aware of their own biases in evaluation. For example, when selecting appropriate story endings, annotators are not operating with a "view from nowhere" but from particular values and circumstances (Nagel, 1989). The positionality of the researchers should also be considered in relation to the narrative authors; the authors' positions are often lost in NLP datasets, even when those datasets are labeled with internal states (e.g., sentiment) known only to the authors. Classifying internal states carries risks (Stark, 2018), which are compounded in the study of personal narratives, where affect, relationships, and narratival motivations are intertwined. One strategy to address this challenge is to include the narrative authors in the dataset design (Heuer and Buschek, 2021). And NLP methods can be used to explore the authors' and researchers' positionality by comparing biased linguistic patterns (Bolukbasi et al., 2016; Caliskan et al., 2017) contained in narratives and case notes.

5.4 Openness to Discovery and Disagreement.

Discovery and disagreement are central components to the open research focus in qualitative HCI methods. When designing labeled datasets and shared tasks, NLP can adopt HCI's open approach; rather than constraining the data and labels to a test a single technical ability, decided a priori, NLP researchers can take an open approach—one that allows for complicated labels that emerge from multiple annotators' interpretation of the data. This opportunity to include labeler disagreements has been noted by a large body of work (Inie and Derczynski, 2021), but given the complexity of narrative data and its many intertwining features (Piper et al., 2021), customized labels (e.g., hierarchical) could more realistically represent narratives than artificial benchmarks with limited utility. On the other side, NLP methods like topic modeling can help surface themes and discourses that are not immediately apparent to qualitative coders (Baumer et al., 2017). NLP methods can also be used to to identify outlier narratives whose structure or framing is unusual for the dataset (Antoniak et al., 2019).

6 Conclusion

As both a research tool and as an object of study, narrative datasets have been widely used in both NLP and HCI. This short work is not intended to describe all approaches to narrative in these disciplines, nor is it intended to provide solutions to all the described challenges. Boundaries between disciplines are fluid, especially in regards to stories shared on social media, where platform design, moderation, and many other HCI concepts have shaped the stories studied via computational NLP methods. Many different fields (e.g., literary studies) are concerned with narratives; we have constrained our discussion to datasets in NLP and qualitative HCI because we see room for cross-pollination and conversations. Stories can be powerful tools of persuasion and expression, and richer methods that draw from both NLP and HCI can raise new questions and open up new directions.

7 Acknowledgements

Thank you to our anonymous reviewers, whose comments were very helpful in preparing this paper. We also thank Sharifa Sultana's Facebook Fellowship for supporting this work.

References

Nader Akoury, Shufan Wang, Josh Whiting, Stephen Hood, Nanyun Peng, and Mohit Iyyer. 2020. STORIUM: A Dataset and Evaluation Platform for Machine-in-the-Loop Story Generation. In *Proceedings of the 2020 Conference on Empirical Methods in Natural Language Processing (EMNLP)*, pages 6470–6484, Online. Association for Computational Linguistics.

Nazanin Andalibi, Pinar Ozturk, and Andrea Forte. 2017. Sensitive self-disclosures, responses, and social support on instagram: The case of depression. In *Proceedings of the 2017 ACM Conference on Computer Supported Cooperative Work and Social Computing*, CSCW '17, page 1485–1500, New York, NY, USA. Association for Computing Machinery.

Maria Antoniak, David Mimno, and Karen Levy. 2019. Narrative paths and negotiation of power in birth stories. *Proc. ACM Hum.-Comput. Interact.*, 3(CSCW).

Michael Bamberg and Alexandra Georgakopoulou. 2008. Small stories as a new perspective in narrative and identity analysis.

David Bamman, Olivia Lewke, and Anya Mansoor. 2020. An annotated dataset of coreference in English literature. In *Proceedings of the 12th Language Resources and Evaluation Conference*, pages 44–54, Marseille, France. European Language Resources Association.

David Bamman, Brendan O'Connor, and Noah A. Smith. 2013. Learning latent personas of film characters. In *Proceedings of the 51st Annual Meeting of the Association for Computational Linguistics (Volume 1: Long Papers)*, pages 352–361, Sofia, Bulgaria. Association for Computational Linguistics.

David Bamman and Noah A. Smith. 2014. Unsupervised discovery of biographical structure from text. *Transactions of the Association for Computational Linguistics*, 2:363–376.

Jeffrey Bardzell, Shaowen Bardzell, Carl DiSalvo, William Gaver, and Phoebe Sengers. 2012. The humanities and/in hci. In *CHI'12 Extended Abstracts on Human Factors in Computing Systems*, pages 1135–1138.

Eric PS Baumer, David Mimno, Shion Guha, Emily Quan, and Geri K Gay. 2017. Comparing grounded theory and topic modeling: Extreme divergence or unlikely convergence? *Journal of the Association for Information Science and Technology*, 68(6):1397–1410.

Natalya N Bazarova, Yoon Hyung Choi, Victoria Schwanda Sosik, Dan Cosley, and Janis Whitlock. 2015. Social sharing of emotions on facebook: Channel differences, satisfaction, and replies. In *Proceedings of the 18th ACM conference on computer supported cooperative work & social computing*, pages 154–164.

Emily M. Bender, Timnit Gebru, Angelina McMillan-Major, and Shmargaret Shmitchell. 2021. On the dangers of stochastic parrots: Can language models be too big? In *Proceedings of the 2021 ACM Conference on Fairness, Accountability, and Transparency*, FAccT '21, page 610–623, New York, NY, USA. Association for Computing Machinery.

Tolga Bolukbasi, Kai-Wei Chang, James Y Zou, Venkatesh Saligrama, and Adam T Kalai. 2016. Man is to computer programmer as woman is to homemaker? Debiasing word embeddings. In *Advances in Neural Information Processing Systems*, pages 4349–4357.

Jerome Bruner. 1987. Life as narrative. *Social research*, pages 11–32.

Jerome Bruner. 1990. Acts of meaning.

Aylin Caliskan, Joanna J Bryson, and Arvind Narayanan. 2017. Semantics derived automatically from language corpora contain human-like biases. *Science*, 356(6334):183–186.

Nathanael Chambers and Dan Jurafsky. 2008. Unsupervised learning of narrative event chains. In *Proceedings of ACL-08: HLT*, pages 789–797, Columbus, Ohio. Association for Computational Linguistics.

Nathanael Chambers and Dan Jurafsky. 2009. Unsupervised learning of narrative schemas and their participants. In *Proceedings of the Joint Conference of the 47th Annual Meeting of the ACL and the 4th International Joint Conference on Natural Language Processing of the AFNLP*, pages 602–610, Suntec, Singapore. Association for Computational Linguistics.

John W Creswell and Vicki L Plano Clark. 2017. *Designing and conducting mixed methods research*. Sage Publications.

Jacob Devlin, Ming-Wei Chang, Kenton Lee, and Kristina Toutanova. 2019. BERT: Pre-training of deep bidirectional transformers for language understanding. In *Proceedings of the 2019 Conference of the North American Chapter of the Association for Computational Linguistics: Human Language Technologies, Volume 1 (Long and Short Papers)*, pages 4171–4186, Minneapolis, Minnesota. Association for Computational Linguistics.

Jessica L Feuston and Anne Marie Piper. 2019. Everyday experiences: small stories and mental illness on instagram. In *Proceedings of the 2019 CHI conference on human factors in computing systems*, pages 1–14.

Leo Gao, Stella Biderman, Sid Black, Laurence Golding, Travis Hoppe, Charles Foster, Jason Phang, Horace He, Anish Thite, Noa Nabeshima, et al. 2020. The pile: An 800gb dataset of diverse text for language modeling. *arXiv preprint arXiv:2101.00027*.

Timnit Gebru, Jamie Morgenstern, Briana Vecchione, Jennifer Wortman Vaughan, Hanna Wallach, Hal Daumé III, and Kate Crawford. 2021. Datasheets for datasets. *Commun. ACM*, 64(12):86–92.

Seraphina Goldfarb-Tarrant, Tuhin Chakrabarty, Ralph Weischedel, and Nanyun Peng. 2020. Content planning for neural story generation with aristotelian rescoring. In *Proceedings of the 2020 Conference on Empirical Methods in Natural Language Processing (EMNLP)*, pages 4319–4338, Online. Association for Computational Linguistics.

Connie Golsteijn and Serena Wright. 2013. Using narrative research and portraiture to inform design research. In *IFIP Conference on Human-Computer Interaction*, pages 298–315. Springer.

Andrew Gordon and Reid Swanson. 2009. Identifying personal stories in millions of weblog entries. In *Third International Conference on Weblogs and Social Media, Data Challenge Workshop, San Jose, CA*, volume 46.

Amit Goyal, Ellen Riloff, and Hal Daumé III. 2010. Automatically producing plot unit representations for narrative text. In *Proceedings of the 2010 Conference on Empirical Methods in Natural Language Processing*, pages 77–86, Cambridge, MA. Association for Computational Linguistics.

Jian Guan, Fei Huang, Zhihao Zhao, Xiaoyan Zhu, and Minlie Huang. 2020. A knowledge-enhanced pretraining model for commonsense story generation. *Transactions of the Association for Computational Linguistics*, 8:93–108.

Hendrik Heuer and Daniel Buschek. 2021. Methods for the design and evaluation of HCI+NLP systems. In *Proceedings of the First Workshop on Bridging Human–Computer Interaction and Natural Language Processing*, pages 28–33, Online. Association for Computational Linguistics.

Nanna Inie and Leon Derczynski. 2021. An IDR framework of opportunities and barriers between HCI and NLP. In *Proceedings of the First Workshop on Bridging Human–Computer Interaction and Natural Language Processing*, pages 101–108, Online. Association for Computational Linguistics.

Mohit Iyyer, Anupam Guha, Snigdha Chaturvedi, Jordan Boyd-Graber, and Hal Daumé III. 2016. Feuding families and former Friends: Unsupervised learning for dynamic fictional relationships. In *Proceedings of the 2016 Conference of the North American Chapter of the Association for Computational Linguistics: Human Language Technologies*, pages 1534–1544, San Diego, California. Association for Computational Linguistics.

Bram Jans, Steven Bethard, Ivan Vulić, and Marie Francine Moens. 2012. Skip n-grams and ranking functions for predicting script events. In *Proceedings of the 13th Conference of the European Chapter of the Association for Computational Linguistics*, pages 336–344, Avignon, France. Association for Computational Linguistics.

Wendy G. Lehnert. 1981. Plot units and narrative summarization. *Cognitive Science*, 5:293–331.

Li Lucy and David Bamman. 2021. Characterizing English variation across social media communities with BERT. *Transactions of the Association for Computational Linguistics*, 9:538–556.

Stephanie Lukin, Kevin Bowden, Casey Barackman, and Marilyn Walker. 2016. PersonaBank: A corpus of personal narratives and their story intention graphs. pages 1026–1033.

Ronald A McQueen and Christina Knussen. 2002. *Research methods for social science: A practical introduction*. Pearson Education.

Erin L Merz, Rina S Fox, and Vanessa L Malcarne. 2014. Expressive writing interventions in cancer patients: A systematic review. *Health Psychology Review*, 8(3):339–361.

Nusrat Jahan Mim and Syed Ishtiaque Ahmed. 2020. Others' images: Online social media, architectural improvisations, and spatial marginalization in bangladesh. In *Proceedings of the 2020 CHI Conference on Human Factors in Computing Systems*, pages 1–14.

Nasrin Mostafazadeh, Nathanael Chambers, Xiaodong He, Devi Parikh, Dhruv Batra, Lucy Vanderwende, Pushmeet Kohli, and James Allen. 2016. A corpus and cloze evaluation for deeper understanding of commonsense stories. In *Proceedings of the 2016 Conference of the North American Chapter of the Association for Computational Linguistics: Human Language Technologies*, pages 839–849, San Diego, California. Association for Computational Linguistics.

Thomas Nagel. 1989. *The view from nowhere*. oxford university press.

Pok-Ja Oh and Soo Hyun Kim. 2016. The effects of expressive writing interventions for patients with cancer: A meta-analysis. In *Oncology Nursing Forum*, volume 43.

Jessica Ouyang and Kathy McKeown. 2014. Towards automatic detection of narrative structure. In *Proceedings of the Ninth International Conference on Language Resources and Evaluation (LREC-2014)*, pages 4624–4631, Reykjavik, Iceland. European Languages Resources Association (ELRA).

James W Pennebaker. 1997. Writing about emotional experiences as a therapeutic process. *Psychological Science*, 8(3):162–166.

James W Pennebaker and Sandra K Beall. 1986. Confronting a traumatic event: toward an understanding of inhibition and disease. *Journal of Abnormal Psychology*, 95(3):274.

Andrew Piper, Richard Jean So, and David Bamman. 2021. Narrative theory for computational narrative understanding. In *Proceedings of the 2021 Conference on Empirical Methods in Natural Language Processing*, pages 298–311, Online and Punta Cana, Dominican Republic. Association for Computational Linguistics.

Andrew J. Reagan, Lewis Mitchell, Dilan Kiley, Christopher M. Danforth, and Peter Sheridan Dodds. 2016. The emotional arcs of stories are dominated by six basic shapes. *EPJ Data Science*, 5:1–12.

Matthew Richardson, Christopher J.C. Burges, and Erin Renshaw. 2013. MCTest: A challenge dataset for the open-domain machine comprehension of text. In *Proceedings of the 2013 Conference on Empirical Methods in Natural Language Processing*, pages 193–203, Seattle, Washington, USA. Association for Computational Linguistics.

Shruti Sannon, Elizabeth L Murnane, Natalya N Bazarova, and Geri Gay. 2019. " i was really, really nervous posting it" communicating about invisible chronic illnesses across social media platforms. In *Proceedings of the 2019 CHI conference on human factors in computing systems*, pages 1–13.

Maarten Sap, Eric Horvitz, Yejin Choi, Noah A. Smith, and James Pennebaker. 2020. Recollection versus imagination: Exploring human memory and cognition via neural language models. In *Proceedings of the 58th Annual Meeting of the Association for Computational Linguistics*, pages 1970–1978, Online. Association for Computational Linguistics.

Roger C Schank and Robert P Abelson. 1977. Scripts, plans, goals, and understanding: An inquiry into human knowledge structures.

Sanket S Sharma and Munmun De Choudhury. 2015. Measuring and characterizing nutritional information of food and ingestion content in instagram. In *Proceedings of the 24th International Conference on World Wide Web*, pages 115–116.

Lisa Slevitch. 2011. Qualitative and quantitative methodologies compared: Ontological and epistemological perspectives. *Journal of quality assurance in hospitality & tourism*, 12(1):73–81.

Luke Stark. 2018. Algorithmic psychometrics and the scalable subject. *Social Studies of Science*, 48(2):204–231. PMID: 29726810.

Bruce Sterling. 2009. Cover story design fiction. *Interactions*, 16(3):20–24.

Miriam Sturdee, Makayla Lewis, Angelika Strohmayer, Katta Spiel, Nantia Koulidou, Sarah Fdili Alaoui, and Josh Urban Davis. 2021. A plurality of practices: artistic narratives in hci research. In *Creativity and Cognition*, pages 1–1.

Sharifa Sultana and Syed Ishtiaque Ahmed. 2019. Witchcraft and hci: Morality, modernity, and postcolonial computing in rural bangladesh. In *Proceedings of the 2019 CHI Conference on Human Factors in Computing Systems*, pages 1–15.

Sharifa Sultana, Mitrasree Deb, Ananya Bhattacharjee, Shaid Hasan, SM Raihanul Alam, Trishna Chakraborty, Prianka Roy, Samira Fairuz Ahmed,

Aparna Moitra, M Ashraful Amin, et al. 2021. 'un-mochon': A tool to combat online sexual harassment over facebook messenger. In *Proceedings of the 2021 CHI Conference on Human Factors in Computing Systems*, pages 1–18.

Timothy R Tangherlini. 2000. Heroes and lies: Storytelling tactics among paramedics. *Folklore*, 111(1):43–66.

Gareth Williams. 1984. The genesis of chronic illness: narrative re-construction. *Sociology of health & illness*, 6(2):175–200.

Peter Wright and John McCarthy. 2004. *Technology as experience*. MIT Press Cambridge.

Peter Wright and John McCarthy. 2008. Empathy and experience in hci. In *Proceedings of the SIGCHI conference on human factors in computing systems*, pages 637–646.

Justine Zhang, William Hamilton, Cristian Danescu-Niculescu-Mizil, Dan Jurafsky, and Jure Leskovec. 2017. Community identity and user engagement in a multi-community landscape. *Proceedings of the International AAAI Conference on Web and Social Media*, 11(1):377–386.

Renwen Zhang, Natalya N. Bazarova, and Madhu Reddy. 2021. Distress disclosure across social media platforms during the covid-19 pandemic: Untangling the effects of platforms, affordances, and audiences. In *Proceedings of the 2021 CHI Conference on Human Factors in Computing Systems*, pages 1–15.

Towards a Deep Multi-layered Dialectal Language Analysis: A Case Study of African-American English

Jamell Dacon
Michigan State University
East Lansing, MI, USA
daconjam@msu.edu

Abstract

Currently, natural language processing (NLP) models proliferate language discrimination leading to potentially harmful societal impacts as a result of biased outcomes. For example, part-of-speech taggers trained on Mainstream American English (MAE) produce non-interpretable results when applied to African American English (AAE) as a result of language features not seen during training. In this work, we incorporate a human-in-the-loop paradigm to gain a better understanding of AAE speakers' behavior and their language use, and highlight the need for dialectal language inclusivity so that native AAE speakers can extensively interact with NLP systems while reducing feelings of disenfranchisement.

1 Introduction

Over the years, social media users have leveraged online conversational platforms to perpetually express themselves online. For example, African American English (AAE)[1], an English language variety is often heavily used on Twitter (Field et al., 2021; Blodgett et al., 2020). This dialect continuum is neither spoken by *all* African Americans or individuals who identify as BIPOC (Black, Indigenous, or People of Color), nor is it spoken *only* by African Americans or BIPOC individuals (Field et al., 2021; Bland-Stewart, 2005). In some cases, AAE, a low-resource language (LRL) may be the first (or dominant) language, rather than the second (or non-dominant) language of an English speaker.

Specifically, AAE is a regional dialect continuum that consists of a distinct set of lexical items, some of which have distinct semantic meanings, and may possess different syntactic structures/patterns than in Mainstream American English (MAE) (*e.g.*, differentiating habitual *be* and non-habitual *be* usage) (Stewart, 2014; Dorn, 2019; Jones, 2015; Field et al., 2021; Bland-Stewart, 2005; Baugh, 2008; Blodgett et al., 2020; Labov, 1975). In particular, Green (2002) states that AAE possesses a morphologically invariant form of the verb that distinguishes between habitual action and currently occurring action, namely *habitual* ***be***. For example, "the habitual be" experiment[2] by University of Massachusetts Amherst's Janice Jackson.

However, AAE is perceived to be "bad english" despite numerous studies by socio/raciolinguists and dialectologists in their attempts to quantify AAE as a legitimized language (Baugh, 2008; Field et al., 2021; Bland-Stewart, 2005; Labov, 1975).

> *"[T]he common misconception [is] that language use has primarily to do with words and what they mean. It doesn't. It has primarily to do with people and what* ***they*** *mean."* – Clark and Schober (1992)

Recently, online AAE has influenced the generation of resources for AAE-like text for natural language (NLP) and corpus linguistic tasks *e.g.*, part-of-speech (POS) tagging (Jørgensen et al., 2016; Blodgett et al., 2018), language generation (Groenwold et al., 2020) and automatic speech recognition (Dorn, 2019; Tatman and Kasten, 2017). POS tagging is a token-level text classification task where each token is assigned a corresponding word category label (see Table 1). It is an enabling tool for NLP applications such as a syntactic parsing, named entity recognition, corpus linguistics, etc. In this work, we incorporate a human-in-the-loop paradigm by directly involving affected (user) communities to understand context and word ambigu-

[1] A dialectal continuum previously known as Northern Negro English, Black English Vernacular (BEV), Black English, African American Vernacular English (AAVE), African American Language (AAL), Ebonics, and Non-standard English (Labov, 1975; Bailey et al., 1998; Green, 2002, 2014; Baugh, 2008; Bland-Stewart, 2005; King, 2020). It is often referred to as African American Language (AAL) and African American English (AAE). In this work, we use the denotation AAE.

[2] https://www.umass.edu/synergy/fall98/ebonics3.html

Proceedings of the Second Workshop on Bridging Human–Computer Interaction and Natural Language Processing, pages 55 - 63
July 15, 2022

MAE	**Input**	I have never done this before
	Output	(I, <PRP>), (have, <VBP>), (never, <RB>), (done, <VBN>), (that, <IN>), (before, <IN>)
AAE	**Input**	I aint neva did dat befo
	Output	(I, <PRP>), (aint, < VBP >), (neva, < NN >), (did, <VBD>)(dat, < JJ >), (befo, < NN >)

Table 1: An illustrative example of POS tagging of semantically equivalent sentences written in MAE and AAE. Each blue and red highlight corresponds to linguistics features of AAE lexical items, and their misclassified NLTK (inferred) tags, respectively.

ities in an attempt to study dialectal language inclusivity in NLP language technologies that are generally designed for dominant language varieties. Dacon and Liu (2021) state that,

> *"NLP systems aim to [learn] from natural language data, and mitigating social biases become a compelling matter not only for machine learning (ML) but for social justice as well."*

To address these issues, we aim to empirically study *predictive bias* (see Swinton (1981) for definition) *i.e.*, if POS tagger models make predictions dependent on demographic language features, and attempt a dynamic approach in data-collection of non-standard spellings and lexical items. To examine the behaviors of AAE speakers and their language use, we first collect variable (morphological and phonological) rules of AAE language features from literature (Labov, 1975; Bailey et al., 1998; Green, 2002; Bland-Stewart, 2005; Stewart, 2014; Blodgett et al., 2016; Elazar and Goldberg, 2018; Baugh, 2008; Green, 2014) (see Appendix C). Then, we employ 5 trained sociolinguist Amazon Mechanical Turk (AMT) annotators[3] who identify as bi-dialectal dominant AAE speakers to address the issue of lexical, semantic and syntactic ambiguity of tweets (see Appendix B for annotation guidelines). Next, we incorporate a human-in-the-loop paradigm by recruiting 20 crowd-sourced diglossic annotators to evaluate AAE language variety (see Table 2). Finally, we conclude by expanding on the need for dialectal language inclusivity.

2 Related Work

Previous works regarding AAE linguistic features have analyzed tasks such as unsupervised domain adaptation for AAE-like language (Jørgensen et al., 2016), detecting AAE syntax(Stewart, 2014), language identification (Blodgett and O'Connor, 2017), voice recognition and transcription (Dorn, 2019), dependency parsing (Blodgett et al., 2018), dialogue systems (Liu et al., 2020), hate speech/toxic language detection and examining racial bias (Sap et al., 2019; Halevy et al., 2021; Xia et al., 2020; Davidson and Bhattacharya, 2020; Zhou et al., 2021; Mozafari et al., 2020; Xu et al., 2021; Koenecke et al., 2020), and language generation (Groenwold et al., 2020). These central works are conclusive for highlighting systematic biases of natural language processing (NLP) systems when employing AAE in common downstream tasks.

Although we mention popular works incorporating AAE, this dialectal continuum has been largely ignored and underrepresented by the NLP community in comparison to MAE. Such lack of language diversity cases constitutes technological inequality to minority groups, for example, by African Americans or BIPOC individuals, and may intensify feelings of disenfranchisement due to monolingualism. We refer to this pitfall as the *inconvenient truth i.e.*,

> *"[If] the systems show discriminatory behaviors in the interactions, the user experience will be adversely affected."* — Liu et al. (2020)

Therefore, we define fairness as the model's ability to correctly predict each tag while performing zero-shot transfer via dialectal language inclusivity.

Moreover, these aforementioned works do not discuss nor reflect on the *"role of the speech and language technologies in sustaining language use"* (Labov, 1975; Bird, 2020; Blodgett et al., 2020) as,

> *"... models are expected to make predictions with the semantic information rather than with the demographic group identity information"* — Zhang et al. (2020).

Interactions with everyday items is increasingly mediated through language, yet systems have limited ability to process less-represented dialects such as AAE. For example, a common AAE phrase, *"I had a long **ass** day"* would receive a lower sentiment polarity score because of the word *"**ass**"*, a (noun) term typically classified as offensive; however, in AAE, this term is often used as an emphatic, cumulative adjective and perceived as non-offensive.

[3]A HIT approval rate $\geq$ 95% was used to select 5 bi-dialectal AMT annotators between the ages of 18 - 55, and completed $>$ 10,000 HITs and located within the United States.

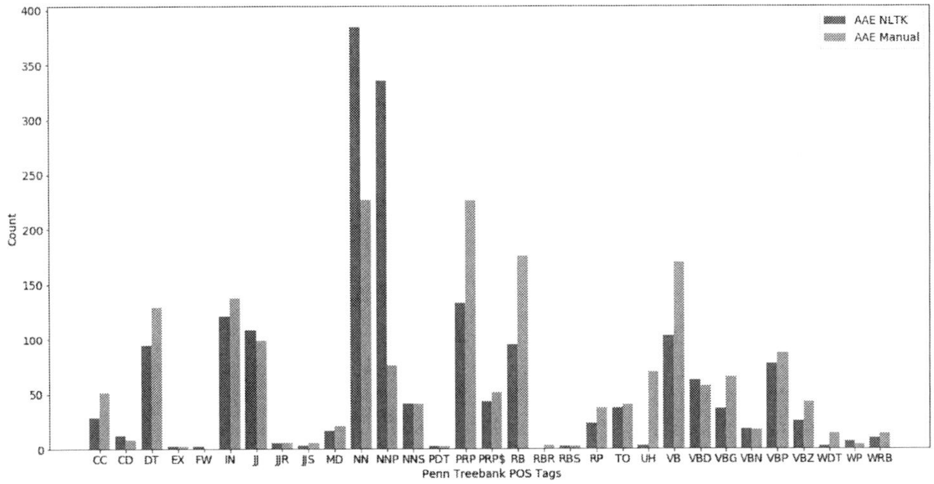

Figure 1: An illustration of inferred and manually-annotated AAE tag counts from k randomly sampled tweets.

Motivation: We want to test our hypothesis that training each model on correctly tagged AAE language features will improve the model's performance, interpretability, explainability, and usability to reduce predictive bias.

3 Dataset and Annotation

3.1 Dataset

We collect 3000 demographically-aligned African American (AA) tweets possessing an average of 7 words per tweet from the publicly available TwitterAAE corpus by Blodgett et al. (2016). Each tweet is accompanied by inferred geolocation topic model probabilities from Twitter + Census demographics and word likelihoods to calculate demographic dialect proportions. We aim to minimize (linguistic) discrimination by sampling tweets that possess over 99% confidence to develop "fair" NLP tools that are originally designed for dominant language varieties by integrating non-standardized varieties. More information about the TwitterAAE dataset, including its statistical information, annotation process, and the link(s) to downloadable versions can be found in Appendix A.

3.2 Preprocessing

As it is common for most words on social media to be plausibly semantically equivalent, we denoise each tweet as tweets typically possess unusual spelling patterns, repeated letter, emoticons and emojis[4]. We replace sequences of multiple repeated letters with three repeated letters (*e.g.*, *Hmmmmmmmm* $\rightarrow$ *Hmmm*), and remove all punctuation, "@" handles of users and emojis. Essentially, we aim to denoise each tweet only to capture non-standard spellings and lexical items more efficiently.

3.3 Annotation

First, we employ off-the-shelf taggers such as spacy[5] and TwitterNLP[6]; however, the Natural Language Toolkit (NLTK) (Loper and Bird, 2002) provides a more fine-grained Penn Treebank Tagset (PTB)[7] along with evaluation metrics per tag such as F1 score. Next, we focus on aggregating the appropriate tags by collecting and manually-annotating tags from AAE/slang-specific dictionaries to assist the AMT annotators, and later we contrast these aggregated tags with inferred NLTK PTB inferred tags. In Figure 1, we display NLTK inferred and manually-annotated AAE tags from $k = 300$ randomly sampled tweets.

- **The Online Slang Dictionary** (American, English, and Urban slang)[8] - created in 1996, this is the oldest web dictionary of slang words, neologisms, idioms, aphorisms, jargon, informal speech, and figurative usages. This dic-

[4]Emoticons are particular textual features made of punctuation such as exclamation marks, letters, and/or numbers to create pictorial icons to display an emotion or sentiment (*e.g.*, ";)" $\Rightarrow$ *winking smile*), while emojis are small text-like pictographs of faces, objects, symbols, etc.

[5]`https://spacy.io`

[6]`https://github.com/ianozsvald/ark-tweet-nlp-python`

[7]`https://www.guru99.com/pos-tagging-chunking-nltk.html`

[8]`http://onlineslangdictionary.com`

Tags	Category	AAE Example(s)	MAE Equivalent(s)
CC	Coordinating Conjunction	*doe/tho, n, bt*	*though, and, but*
DT	Determiner	*da, dis, dat*	*the, this, that*
EX	Existential There	*dea*	*there*
IN	Preposition/ Conjunction	*fa, cuz/cause, den*	*for, because, than*
JJ	Adjective	*foine, hawt*	*fine, hot*
PRP	Pronoun	*u, dey, dem*	*you, they, them*
PRP$	Personal Pronoun	*ha*	*her*
RB	Adverb	*tryna, finna, jus*	*trying to, fixing to, just*
RBR	Adverb, comparative	*mo, betta, hotta*	*more, better, hotter*
RP	Particle	*bout, thru*	*about, through*
TO	Infinite marker	*ta*	*to*
UH	Interjection	*wassup, ion, ian*	*what's up, I don't*
VBG	Verb, gerund	*sleepin, gettin*	*sleeping, getting*
VBZ	Verb, 3rd-person present tense	*iz*	*is*
WDT	Wh-determiner	*dat, wat, wus, wen*	*that, what, what's, when*
WRB	Wh-adverb	*hw*	*how*

Table 2: Accurately tagged (observed) AAE and English phonological and morphological **linguistic** feature(s) accompanied by their respective MAE equivalent(s).

tionary possesses more than 24,000 real definitions and tags for over 17,000 slang words and phrases, 600 categories of meaning, word use mapping and aids in addressing lexical ambiguity.

- **Word Type**[9] - an open source POS focused dictionary of words based on the Wiktionary[10] project by Wikimedia[11]. Researchers have parsed Wiktionary and other sources, including real definitions and categorical POS word use cases necessary to address the issue of lexical, semantic and syntactic ambiguity.

3.4 Human Evaluation

After an initial training of the AMT annotators, we task each annotator to annotate each tweet with the appropriate POS tags. Then, as a calibration study we attempt to measure the inter-annotator agreement (IAA) using Krippendorff's α. By using NLTK's (Loper and Bird, 2002) nltk.metrics.agreement, we calculate a Krippendorf's α of 0.88. We did not observe notable distinctions in annotator agreement across the individual tweets. We later randomly sampled 300 annotated tweets and recruit 20 crowd-sourced annotators to evaluate AAE language variety. To recruit 20 diglossic annotators[12], we created a volunteer questionnaire with annotation guildlines, and released it on LinkedIn. The full annotation guildlines can be found in Appendix B. Each recruited annotator is tasked to judge sampled tweets and list their MAE equivalents to examine contextual differences of simple, deterministic morphosyntactic substitutions of dialect-specific vocabulary in standard English or MAE texts—a *reverse* study to highlight several varieties of AAE (see Table 2).

4 Methodology

In this section, we describe our approach to perform a preliminary study to validate the existence of predictive bias (Elazar and Goldberg, 2018; Shah et al., 2020) in POS models. We first introduce the POS tagging, and then propose two ML sequence models.

4.1 Part-of-Speech (POS) Tagging

We consider POS tagging as it represents word syntactic categories and serves as a pre-annotation tool for numerous downstream tasks, especially for non-standardized English language varieties such as AAE (Zampieri et al., 2020). Common tags include prepositions, adjective, pronoun, noun, adverb, verb, interjection, etc., where multiple POS tags can be assigned to particular words due to syntactic structural patterns. This can also lead to misclassification of non-standardized words that do not exist in popular pre-trained NLP models.

4.2 Models

We propose to implement two well known sequence modeling algorithms, namely a Bidirectional

[9] `https://wordtype.org/`
[10] `https://www.wiktionary.org`
[11] `https://www.wikimedia.org`
[12] Note that we did not collect certain demographic information such as gender or race, only basic demographics such as age (18-55 years), state and country of residence.

Long Short Term Memory (Bi-LSTM) network, a deep neutral network (DNN) (Hochreiter and Schmidhuber, 1997; Graves and Schmidhuber, 2005) that has been used for POS tagging (Ling et al., 2015; Plank et al., 2016), and a Conditional Random Field (CRF) (Lafferty et al.) typically used to identify entities or patterns in texts by exploiting previously learned word data.

Taggers: First, we use NLTK (Loper and Bird, 2002) for automatic tagging; then, we pre-define a feature function for our CRF model where we optimized its L1 and L2 regularization parameters to 0.25 and 0.3, respectively. Later, we train our Bi-LSTM network for 40 epochs with an Adam optimizer, and a learning rate of 0.001. Note that each model would be accompanied by error analysis for a 70-30 split of the data with 5-fold cross-validation to obtain model classification reports, for metrics such as precision, recall and F1-score.

5 Operationalization of AAE as an English Language Variety

As (online) AAE can incorporate non-standardized spellings and lexical items, there is an active need for a human-in-the-loop paradigm as humans provide various forms of feedback in different stages of workflow. This can significantly improve the model's performance, interpretability, explainability, and usability. Therefore, crowd-sourcing to develop language technologies that consider who created the data will lead to the inclusion of diverse training data, and thus, decrease feelings of marginalization. For example, CORAAL[13], is an online resource that features AAL text data, recorded speech data, etc., into new and existing NLP technologies, AAE speakers can extensively interact with current NLP language technologies.

Consequently, to quantitatively and qualitatively ensure fairness in NLP tools, artificial intelligence (AI) and NLP researchers need to go beyond evaluation measures, word definitions and word order to assess AAE on a token-level to better understand context, culture and word ambiguities. We encourage both AI and NLP practitioners to prioritize collecting a set of relevant labeled training data with several examples of informal phrases, expressions, idioms, and regional-specific varieties. Specifically, in models intended for broad use such as sentiment analysis by partnering with low-resource and dialectal communities to develop impactful speech and language technologies for dialect continua such as AAE to minimize further stigmatization of an already stigmatized minority group.

[13]https://oraal.uoregon.edu/coraal

6 Conclusion

Throughout this work, we highlight the need to develop language technologies for such varieties, pushing back against potentially discriminatory practices (in many cases, discriminatory through oversight more than malice). Our work calls for NLP researchers to consider both social and racial hierarchies sustained or intensified by current computational linguistic research. By shifting towards a human-in-the-loop paradigm to conduct deep multi-layered dialectal language analysis of AAE to counter-attack erasure and several forms of biases such as *selection bias*, *label bias*, *model overamplification*, and *semantic bias* (see Shah et al. (2020) for definitions) in NLP.

We hope our dynamic approach can encourage practitioners, researchers and developers for AAE inclusive work, and that our contributions can pave the way for normalizing the use of a human-in-the-loop paradigm both to obtain new data and create NLP tools to better comprehend underrepresented dialect continua and English language varieties. In this way, NLP community can revolutionize the ways in which humans and technology cooperate by considering certain demographic attributes such as culture, background, race and gender when developing and deploying NLP models.

7 Limitations And Ethical Considerations

All authors must warrant that increased model performance for non-standard varieties such as underrepresented dialects, non-standard spellings or lexical items in NLP systems can potentially enable automated discrimination. In this work, we *solely* attempt to highlight the need for dialectal inclusivity for the development of impactful speech and language technologies in the future, and do not intend for increased feelings of marginalization of an already stigmatized community.

8 Acknowledgements

The authors would like to thank Shaylnn L.A. Crum-Dacon, Serena Lotreck, Brianna Brown and Kenia Segura Abá, Jyothi Kumar and Shin-Han Shiu for their support and the anonymous reviewers for their constructive comments.

References

Guy Bailey, John Baugh, Salikoko S. Mufwene, and John R. Rickford. 1998. *African-American English: Structure, History and Use (1st ed.)*. Routledge.

John Baugh. 2008. Linguistic discrimination. In *1. Halbband*, pages 709–714. De Gruyter Mouton.

Steven Bird. 2020. Decolonising speech and language technology. In *Proceedings of the 28th International Conference on Computational Linguistics*, pages 3504–3519, Barcelona, Spain (Online). International Committee on Computational Linguistics.

Linda M. Bland-Stewart. 2005. Difference or deficit in speakers of african american english? `https://leader.pubs.asha.org/doi/10.1044/leader.FTR1.10062005.6`.

Su Lin Blodgett, Solon Barocas, Hal Daumé III, and Hanna Wallach. 2020. Language (technology) is power: A critical survey of "bias" in NLP. In *Proceedings of the 58th Annual Meeting of the Association for Computational Linguistics*, pages 5454–5476, Online. Association for Computational Linguistics.

Su Lin Blodgett, Lisa Green, and Brendan O'Connor. 2016. Demographic dialectal variation in social media: A case study of African-American English. In *Proceedings of the 2016 Conference on Empirical Methods in Natural Language Processing*, pages 1119–1130, Austin, Texas. Association for Computational Linguistics.

Su Lin Blodgett and Brendan O'Connor. 2017. Racial disparity in natural language processing: A case study of social media african-american english. *CoRR*, abs/1707.00061.

Su Lin Blodgett, Johnny Wei, and Brendan O'Connor. 2018. Twitter Universal Dependency parsing for African-American and mainstream American English. In *Proceedings of the 56th Annual Meeting of the Association for Computational Linguistics (Volume 1: Long Papers)*, pages 1415–1425, Melbourne, Australia. Association for Computational Linguistics.

Herbert H. Clark and Michael F. Schober. 1992. Asking questions and influencing answers. In *Russell Sage Foundation*.

Jamell Dacon and Haochen Liu. 2021. Does gender matter in the news? detecting and examining gender bias in news articles. In *Companion Proceedings of the Web Conference 2021*, WWW '21, page 385–392, New York, NY, USA. Association for Computing Machinery.

Thomas Davidson and Debasmita Bhattacharya. 2020. Examining racial bias in an online abuse corpus with structural topic modeling. *CoRR*, abs/2005.13041.

Rachel Dorn. 2019. Dialect-specific models for automatic speech recognition of African American Vernacular English. In *Proceedings of the Student Research Workshop Associated with RANLP 2019*, pages 16–20, Varna, Bulgaria. INCOMA Ltd.

Yanai Elazar and Yoav Goldberg. 2018. Adversarial removal of demographic attributes from text data. In *Proceedings of the 2018 Conference on Empirical Methods in Natural Language Processing*, pages 11–21, Brussels, Belgium. Association for Computational Linguistics.

Anjalie Field, Su Lin Blodgett, Zeerak Waseem, and Yulia Tsvetkov. 2021. A survey of race, racism, and anti-racism in NLP. *CoRR*, abs/2106.11410.

Alex Graves and Jürgen Schmidhuber. 2005. Framewise phoneme classification with bidirectional lstm and other neural network architectures. *Neural Networks*, 18(5):602–610. IJCNN 2005.

Jonathon Green. 2014. *The vulgar tongue: Green's history of slang*. Oxford University Press, New York, USA.

Lisa J. Green. 2002. *African American English: A Linguistic Introduction*. Cambridge University Press.

Sophie Groenwold, Lily Ou, Aesha Parekh, Samhita Honnavalli, Sharon Levy, Diba Mirza, and William Yang Wang. 2020. Investigating African-American Vernacular English in transformer-based text generation. In *Proceedings of the 2020 Conference on Empirical Methods in Natural Language Processing (EMNLP)*, pages 5877–5883, Online. Association for Computational Linguistics.

Matan Halevy, Camille Harris, Amy Bruckman, Diyi Yang, and Ayanna Howard. 2021. Mitigating racial biases in toxic language detection with an equity-based ensemble framework. New York, NY, USA. Association for Computing Machinery.

Sepp Hochreiter and Jürgen Schmidhuber. 1997. Long short-term memory. *Neural Comput.*, 9(8):1735–1780.

Taylor Jones. 2015. Toward a description of african american vernacular english dialect regions using "black twitter". *American Speech*, 90:403–440.

Anna Jørgensen, Dirk Hovy, and Anders Søgaard. 2016. Learning a POS tagger for AAVE-like language. In *Proceedings of the 2016 Conference of the North American Chapter of the Association for Computational Linguistics: Human Language Technologies*, pages 1115–1120, San Diego, California. Association for Computational Linguistics.

Sharese King. 2020. From african american vernacular english to african american language: Rethinking the study of race and language in african americans' speech. *Annual Review of Linguistics*, 6(1):285–300.

Allison Koenecke, Andrew Nam, Emily Lake, Joe Nudell, Minnie Quartey, Zion Mengesha, Connor Toups, John R. Rickford, Dan Jurafsky, and Sharad

Goel. 2020. Racial disparities in automated speech recognition. *Proceedings of the National Academy of Sciences*, 117(14):7684–7689.

William Labov. 1975. Ralph fasold, tense marking in black english: a linguistic and social analysis. washington, d.c.: Center for applied linguistics, 1972. pp. 254. *Language in Society*, 4(2):222–227.

John Lafferty, Andrew McCallum, and Fernando CN Pereira. Conditional random fields: Probabilistic models for segmenting and labeling sequence data.

Wang Ling, Chris Dyer, Alan W Black, Isabel Trancoso, Ramón Fermandez, Silvio Amir, Luís Marujo, and Tiago Luís. 2015. Finding function in form: Compositional character models for open vocabulary word representation. In *Proceedings of the 2015 Conference on Empirical Methods in Natural Language Processing*, pages 1520–1530, Lisbon, Portugal. Association for Computational Linguistics.

Haochen Liu, Jamell Dacon, Wenqi Fan, Hui Liu, Zitao Liu, and Jiliang Tang. 2020. Does gender matter? towards fairness in dialogue systems. In *Proceedings of the 28th International Conference on Computational Linguistics*, pages 4403–4416, Barcelona, Spain (Online). International Committee on Computational Linguistics.

Edward Loper and Steven Bird. 2002. NLTK: The natural language toolkit. In *Proceedings of the ACL-02 Workshop on Effective Tools and Methodologies for Teaching Natural Language Processing and Computational Linguistics*, pages 63–70, Philadelphia, Pennsylvania, USA. Association for Computational Linguistics.

Marzieh Mozafari, Reza Farahbakhsh, and Noël Crespi. 2020. Hate speech detection and racial bias mitigation in social media based on bert model. *PLOS ONE*, 15:1–26.

Barbara Plank, Anders Søgaard, and Yoav Goldberg. 2016. Multilingual part-of-speech tagging with bidirectional long short-term memory models and auxiliary loss. In *Proceedings of the 54th Annual Meeting of the Association for Computational Linguistics (Volume 2: Short Papers)*, pages 412–418, Berlin, Germany. Association for Computational Linguistics.

Maarten Sap, Dallas Card, Saadia Gabriel, Yejin Choi, and Noah A. Smith. 2019. The risk of racial bias in hate speech detection. In *Proceedings of the 57th Annual Meeting of the Association for Computational Linguistics*, pages 1668–1678, Florence, Italy. Association for Computational Linguistics.

Deven Santosh Shah, H. Andrew Schwartz, and Dirk Hovy. 2020. Predictive biases in natural language processing models: A conceptual framework and overview. In *Proceedings of the 58th Annual Meeting of the Association for Computational Linguistics*, pages 5248–5264, Online. Association for Computational Linguistics.

Ian Stewart. 2014. Now we stronger than ever: African-American English syntax in Twitter. In *Proceedings of the Student Research Workshop at the 14th Conference of the European Chapter of the Association for Computational Linguistics*, pages 31–37, Gothenburg, Sweden. Association for Computational Linguistics.

Spencer S. Swinton. 1981. Predictive bias in graduate admissions tests. *ETS Research Report Series*, 1981.

Rachael Tatman and Conner Kasten. 2017. Effects of Talker Dialect, Gender & Race on Accuracy of Bing Speech and YouTube Automatic Captions. In *Proc. Interspeech 2017*, pages 934–938.

Mengzhou Xia, Anjalie Field, and Yulia Tsvetkov. 2020. Demoting racial bias in hate speech detection. In *Proceedings of the Eighth International Workshop on Natural Language Processing for Social Media*, pages 7–14, Online. Association for Computational Linguistics.

Albert Xu, Eshaan Pathak, Eric Wallace, Suchin Gururangan, Maarten Sap, and Dan Klein. 2021. Detoxifying language models risks marginalizing minority voices. In *Proceedings of the 2021 Conference of the North American Chapter of the Association for Computational Linguistics: Human Language Technologies*, pages 2390–2397, Online. Association for Computational Linguistics.

Marcos Zampieri, Preslav Nakov, and Yves Scherrer. 2020. Natural language processing for similar languages, varieties, and dialects: A survey. *Natural Language Engineering*, 26(6):595–612.

Guanhua Zhang, Bing Bai, Junqi Zhang, Kun Bai, Conghui Zhu, and Tiejun Zhao. 2020. Demographics should not be the reason of toxicity: Mitigating discrimination in text classifications with instance weighting. In *Proceedings of the 58th Annual Meeting of the Association for Computational Linguistics*, pages 4134–4145, Online. Association for Computational Linguistics.

Xuhui Zhou, Maarten Sap, Swabha Swayamdipta, Yejin Choi, and Noah Smith. 2021. Challenges in automated debiasing for toxic language detection. In *Proceedings of the 16th Conference of the European Chapter of the Association for Computational Linguistics: Main Volume*, pages 3143–3155, Online. Association for Computational Linguistics.

A Dataset Details

Our collected dataset is demographically-aligned on AAE in correspondence on the dialectal tweet corpus by Blodgett et al. (2016). The Twitter-AAE corpus is publicly available and can be downloaded from link[14]. Blodgett et al. (2016) uses a

[14]http://slanglab.cs.umass.edu/TwitterAAE/

mixed-membership demographic language model which calculates demographic dialect proportions for a text accompanied by a race attribute—African America, Hispanic, Other, and White in that order. The race attribute is annotated by a jointly inferred probabilistic topic model based on the geolocation information of each user and tweet. Given that geolocation information (residence) is highly associated with the race of a user, the model can make accurate predictions. However, there a a low number messages that possess a posterior probabilities of NaN as these are messages that have no in-vocabulary words under the model.

B Annotator Annotation Guidelines

You will be given demographically-aligned African American tweets, in which we refer to these tweets as sequences. As a dominant AAE speaker, who identifies as bi-dialectal, your task is to correctly identify the context of each word in a given sequence in hopes to address the issues of lexical, semantic and syntactic ambiguity.

1. Are you a dominant AAE speaker?

2. If you responded "yes" above, are you bi-dialectal?

3. If you responded "yes", given a sequence, have you ever said, seen or used any of these words given the particular sequence?

4. Given a sequence, what are the SAE equivalents to the identified non-SAE terms?

5. For morphological and phonological (dialectal) purposes, are these particular words spelt how would you say or use them?

6. If you responded "no" above, can you provide a different spelling along with its SAE equivalent?

B.1 Annotation Protocol

1. What is the context of each word given the particular sequence?

2. Given NLTK's Penn Treebank Tagset[15], what is the most appropriate POS tag for each word in the given sequence?

[15] `https://www.guru99.com/pos-tagging-chunking-nltk.html`

B.2 Human evaluation of POS tags Protocol

1. Given the tagged sentence, are there any misclassified tags?

2. If you responded "yes" above, can you provide a different POS tag, and state why it is different?

C Variable Rules Examples

In this section we present a few examples of simple, deterministic phonological and morphological language features or *current* variable rules which highlight several regional varieties of AAE which typically attain misclassified POS tags. Please note that a more exhaustive list of these rules is still being constructed as this work is still ongoing. Below are a few variable cases (MAE → AAE), some of which may have been previously shown in Table 2:

1. Consonant ('**t**') deletion (Adverb case) : e.g. "*just*" → "*jus*"; "*must*" → "*mus*"

2. Contractive negative auxiliary verbs replacement: "*doesn't*" → "*don't*"

3. Contractive (**'re**) loss: e.g. "*you're*" → "*you*"; "*we're*" → "*we*"

4. Copula deletion: Deletion of the verb "**be**" and its variants, namely "**is**" and "**are**" e.g. "*He* **is** *on his way*" → "*He on his way*"; "*You* **are** *right*" → "*You right*"

5. Homophonic word replacement (Pronoun case): e.g. "*you're*" → "*your*"

6. Indefinite pronoun replacement: e.g. "*anyone*" → "*anybody*";

7. Interdental fricative loss (Coordinating Conjuction case): e.g. "*this*" → "*dis*"; '*that*' → '*dat*"; "*the*" → "*da*"

8. Phrase reduction (present/ future tense) ⇒ word (Adverb case): e.g. "*what's up*" → "*wassup*"; "*fixing to*" → "*finna*"

9. Present tense possession replacement: e.g. "*John **has** two apples*" → "*John **got** two apples*"; "*The neighbors **have** a bigger pool*" → "*The neighbors **got** a bigger pool*"

10. Remote past "***been***" + completive ('**done**'): "*I've **already done** that*" → "*I **been done** that*"

11. Remote past "***been***" + completive ('**did**'): "*She **already did** that*" → "*She **been did** that*"

12. Remote past "***been***" + Present tense possession replacement: "***I already have** food*" → "*I **been had** food*"; "*You **already have** those shoes*" → "*You **been got** those shoes*"

13. Term-fragment deletion: e.g. "*brother*" → "*bro*"; "*sister*" → "*sis*"; "*your*" → "*ur*"; "*suppose*" → "*pose*"; "*more*" → "*mo*"

14. Term-fragment replacement: "*something*" → "*sumn*"; "*through*" → "*thru*"; "*for*" → "*fa*"; "*nothing*" → "*nun*"

Author Index